Managing with CBT FOR DUMMIES®

Managing Anxiety with CBT

FOR DUMMIES®

by Graham Davey, Kate Cavanagh, Fergal Jones, Lydia Turner and Adrian Whittington

WILEY

A John Wiley and Sons, Ltd, Publication

Managing Anxiety with CBT For Dummies®

Published by
John Wiley & Sons, Ltd
The Atrium
Southern Gate
Chichester
West Sussex
PO19 8SQ
England
www.wiley.com

This edition first published 2012

For general information on our other products and services, please contact our Customer Care Department within the U.S. at 877-762-2974, outside the U.S. at (001) 317-572-3993, or fax 317-572-4002. For technical support, please visit www.wiley.com/techsupport.

A catalogue record for this book is available from the British Library.

ISBN 978-1-118-36606-6 (pbk), ISBN 978-1-118-36609-7 (ebk),
ISBN 978-1-118-36607-3 (ebk), ISBN 978-1-118-36608-0 (ebk)

Printed in the UK

Contents at a Glance

Table of Contents

Introduction

● ●

Cognitive Behavioural Therapy, or CBT, is one of the most popular modern treatments for psychological problems, and is the treatment of choice for common mental health problems such as anxiety and depression. In this book we help you use the principles and practices of CBT as a tool to help you overcome problematic anxiety.

The strength of CBT is that it helps you to identify patterns in your thoughts and behaviours that exacerbate and maintain your anxiety. CBT then provides basic ways in which you can change unhelpful thinking (the *cognitive*, or thinking, bit), and find new ways to behave (the *behavioural* bit) that minimise anxiety.

You're not unusual if you suffer from anxiety problems. They're a common feature of modern-day living, and sometimes anxiety can overwhelm you. In this book we use tried and tested treatment methods that enable you to overcome your own anxiety. We discuss how normal anxiety can turn into a problem, and the various ways in which problematic anxiety can manifest itself. And we show you how the principles and practices of CBT can help you, and how you can maintain your progress and build a better and fuller life.

About This Book

We wrote this book to provide comprehensible coverage of what anxiety is and how you can use CBT to overcome it. The book covers:

- ✓ Knowing what anxiety is and how it can become a problem.

- ✓ Understanding your own anxiety and drawing up a map of your anxiety that helps you explain what causes it and what maintains it.

- ✓ Setting goals for yourself when starting to deal with your anxiety.

✔ Using techniques for facing up to your fears and anxieties.

✔ Dealing with uncontrollable worrying.

✔ Identifying unhelpful rules you use that maintain your anxiety, and providing you with various techniques to change these rules and 'errors of thinking'.

✔ Putting your anxiety into perspective and helping you to make lifestyle changes that maintain your mental health and ward off anxiety.

We've tried to adopt a simple, readable style, and we've provided interesting activities, examples and illustrations that we hope you find accessible and even entertaining. Most importantly, we hope that you find out a little about CBT and are able to use it in the context of your own life to help you understand and manage your own anxiety.

However, if your anxiety is causing you considerable distress to the point where it's interfering significantly with the things you need to do each day and with your enjoyment of life, then we recommend that you seek professional help to provide you with an additional helping hand.

Conventions Used in This Book

Italics introduce new terms, underscore key differences in meaning between words and highlight the most important aspects of a sentence or example.

Bold text shows keywords and the action part of numbered lists.

Sidebars – the grey shaded boxes you see in most chapters – contain interesting titbits of information or occasionally expand on a topic within the chapter. Read them if they look interesting to you, or skip them.

How This Book Is Organised

We divide the book into four parts consisting of a total of 11 chapters. The table of contents lists subheadings that provide more information about each chapter, but below is a brief description of the purpose and contents of each of the four parts of the book.

Part I: Understanding Your Anxiety

This part helps you to understand what anxiety is and why people experience it.

In Chapter 1 we discuss ways in which people experience anxiety, and cover the physical experience and how anxiety affects your thinking. We explore the question of when anxiety becomes a problem, what forms anxiety takes when it becomes a problem and whether you can learn to overcome your anxiety when it seems to control you. We also introduce you to CBT and how CBT can help you to manage your anxiety.

Chapter 2 then guides you through making a map of your anxiety that helps you to explain what causes it and keeps it going. This map is useful in later chapters because it provides you with a guide to what you need to change.

Part II: Tackling Your Anxiety

We start this part, in Chapter 3, by helping you to think about what goals you set for yourself and where you would like to end up when you've dealt with your anxiety. Chapter 4 provides you with some methods for facing up to your fears and anxieties, and we discuss ways of putting yourself into situations that you've previously been avoiding. Then, in Chapter 5, you put your anxieties into perspective with a few tests to determine whether your fears are real or not.

Chapter 6 gives help in beating that chronic feature of anxiety known as 'worrying'. Persistent worry is one of the main features of anxiety, and overcoming it requires dedicated attention. Finally, everyone lives by rules, and Chapter 7 describes how unrealistic and unhelpful rules for living play a role in anxiety, and describes ways of overcoming these rules.

Part III: Making Progress and Moving On

There's more to you as a person than anxiety! In this part we start, in Chapter 8, by putting your anxiety into perspective by describing some of the common contributing problems, such as low mood, depression, troubled sleep and problems with alcohol or prescription drugs. We also provide you with tips and advice about keeping a healthy lifestyle that helps you keep anxiety at bay. Then, in Chapter 9, we look at how you can move toward a brighter future based on our guidance in the book, building on successes and dodging pitfalls.

Part IV: The Part of Tens

This section contains some quick tips about dealing with anxiety and using CBT. We offer our top tips for tackling anxiety and the best ways to expand your horizons and get on with your life.

Icons Used in This Book

We use the following icons in this book to alert you to various important or helpful types of information:

This icon alerts you to a true-to-life example that helps you understand the point.

Here we provide practical advice for putting CBT into practice or describe an activity that we hope you find useful in helping you to understand your anxiety.

This icon tells you that we're discussing something important, so make sure that you take this issue in and remember it.

Beware! This icon alerts you to red flags and things that you should avoid in order to progress successfully or to develop better emotional health.

Whenever you use CBT to help you with your problems, you engage in specific activities to help you understand the process. This icon provides some examples of things for you to try out.

Where to Go from Here

We hope you enjoy this self-help book and benefit from the journey we lay down for understanding and managing your anxiety. We also hope that you gain a genuine insight into how you can use CBT to deal with common emotional and mental health problems.

If you feel that you cope better with anxiety as a result of using this book, make sure that you build on these successes and move towards a healthier and happier lifestyle.

We wish you well!

Part I

Understanding Your Anxiety

The 5th Wave   By Rich Tennant

"It's just a little device I use to help relieve the anxiety from meeting new people."

In this part . . .

In this part, you learn about the different types of anxiety problems and what causes them. In particular, you discover the role that thoughts and behaviours play in maintaining anxiety problems. We show you how to make a map of your anxiety and give you an overview of how CBT can help.

Chapter 1

All About Anxiety

In This Chapter

▶ Finding out why and how you experience anxiety

▶ Discovering the benefits of anxiety

▶ Knowing when anxiety becomes a problem

▶ Using CBT to alleviate anxiety

*A*nxiety is just one of a number of important emotions that you experience on a daily basis and that have important effects on the way you think and behave. Most importantly, anxiety is an emotion that can have beneficial effects (making you alert and focused when faced with potential challenges) or it can be debilitating and distressing if it takes over your life and feels uncontrollable.

In this chapter we lay the foundations for a thorough understanding of anxiety. We explain what exactly anxiety is, and why and how you experience it. We determine when it is that anxiety becomes a problem, and seems to control you. Finally, we introduce you to cognitive behavioural therapy (CBT): what it is, and how it can help you.

Understanding the Basics of Anxiety

Everyone experiences many emotions on a daily basis. In this section we look at some of those emotions, including anxiety, and explain that emotions – even anxiety – can be useful when experienced at the right time and in the right amount.

Knowing that anxiety is a normal, and useful, emotion

Your feelings have evolved to serve adaptive purposes and, in most cases, they help you to solve problems that you encounter. Here are some important emotions that you experience pretty much daily:

- ✔ Anger in response to feeling challenged or thwarted.
- ✔ Anxiety in response to anticipated threats.
- ✔ Disgust in response to repulsive or sickening things or events.
- ✔ Fear in response to immediate perceived threats.
- ✔ Happiness/joy in response to things that you find positive or rewarding.
- ✔ Sadness/sorrow in response to losses or failures you experience.

In general, positive emotions like joy make you feel good (because you associate them with achievement and reward) and negative emotions like anger tend to feel unpleasant (because you associate then with threats, challenges and losses). Nevertheless, the significance of all emotions is that they help you react to, adapt to and deal more successfully with these various types of life events.

So in the case of anxiety, most people are willing to put up with the unpleasant feeling that anxiety gives them because the emotion helps them to deal more effectively with the threats and challenges they face in day-to-day life. Yes, we're talking about a positive side to anxiety. Table 1-1 provides everyday examples of the advantages of the emotion.

Table 1-1	The Benefits of Anxiety
Threat or Challenge	*Benefits of Anxiety*
Preparing for an interview	Feeling a bit anxious makes you focus on the interview and provides a level of arousal that ensures that you're motivated and alert to answer questions.
Meeting an important person for the first time (for example on a date)	Normal levels of anxiety enable you to think through a few of the things that might happen during the meeting and prepare yourself to deal with these possibilities.
Finding your bank balance is overdrawn	A bit of anxiety focuses you on the problem and helps you to problem-solve how you could get your bank balance back into the black.

Appreciating the purpose of anxiety

To survive as living organisms, people must be able to effectively deal with all those things in the world that are likely to pose threats to survival. Many unsophisticated organisms survive by having biologically pre-wired responses to basic threats. Humans too have some responses they're born with that help them to deal with potential threats. For example, people have pre-wired startle responses that make them suddenly alert to the kinds of things that might signal threats. People are startled by:

✔ Sudden loud noises.

✔ Looming shadows.

✔ Rapid movement of things towards them.

✔ Rapid, unpredictable movements around them.

✔ Staring eyes.

Interestingly, all these things that startle people are also characteristic of potential predators, so the startle response is a primitive one designed to make you alert to, and avoid, physical threat. However, the modern world is made up of many more potential threats and challenges than this, so people have evolved a more flexible system to help them deal with the vast range of threats and challenges that confront them during a normal lifetime. This situation is where anxiety and its various elements comes in as a means of helping you to deal with anything that you've labelled as threatening.

So, if you've thought about something and decided – for whatever reason – that it's potentially threatening, you begin to experience anxiety as an emotion that helps you deal with this perceived threat by making you more alert and focused.

The more things you interpret as threatening, the more anxiety you experience. So, the more you tend to interpret events as threats, the more anxious you feel.

Experiencing anxiety

You experience anxiety in a variety of ways:

- ✓ **Feelings:** You experience an unpleasant feeling of apprehension (as if you're under threat).

- ✓ **Bodily sensations:** You may have tense muscles and a dry mouth, a shirt stuck to you with sweat, and be trembling and struggling to swallow.

- ✓ **Physiological changes:** Your heart beats faster, you feel more alert and vigilant, and your reactions are faster.

- ✓ **Behaviours:** You want to avoid the source of what's making you anxious.

- ✓ **Thoughts:** Perhaps paradoxically (given how unpleasant anxiety can make you feel), anxiety makes you think more closely and more directly about threats and challenges. Anxiety can affect your thinking by:

  - • **Controlling your attention:** Anxiety forces you to focus things on that may be threatening or problematic.

  - • **Determining how you interpret things:** If something could be good or bad, anxiety compels you to adopt the bad interpretation.

- **Affecting your reasoning:** Anxiety makes you search for reasons that things might be bad or problematic.

- **Making you think that things are worse than they really are:** This *catastrophising* causes you to make mountains out of molehills.

- **Making you expect bad things happening:** You think life will hand you lemons more often than in fact it does.

The relationship between anxiety and thinking works both ways – anxiety can affect the way you think, but the way you think can also cause you to feel anxious. So if you're not careful, the interaction between thoughts and feelings can spiral out of control and leave you with distressing levels of anxiety.

All these elements form the basis of *normally experienced anxiety*. As we emphasise throughout this book, normally experienced anxiety is an unpleasant feeling, but in most cases is a short-lived experience and one that's a common reaction to future threats and challenges. In proper amounts, normally experienced anxiety is adaptive and beneficial.

Knowing When Anxiety Becomes a Problem

Anxiety is an emotion that serves a purpose in specific situations. Even though anxiety isn't necessarily a pleasant experience, most people can usually control it. They turn on the emotion when necessary, and then turn if off when they no longer need it. But some people lose their ability to manage their anxiety, and it begins to become a regular unpleasant experience. Anxiety becomes a relatively pervasive emotion that they experience on a regular basis, from waking up in the morning to going to bed at night.

So how does anxiety change from being a benefit to a problem?

Seeing how anxiety takes over

A number of factors can make your anxiety seem uncontrollable:

- **Awareness:** You become overly aware of your feelings of anxiety when they occur and focus on them to the point where this attention to the feelings just makes them feel worse.

- **Rules and beliefs:** You develop rules and beliefs that you must do certain things when you encounter something that's threatening or challenging, and these act to maintain anxiety. Examples include:

  - 'Worry is a necessary thing to do.'

  - 'I must resolve all uncertainty.'

  - 'If anything bad happens it will be my fault, so I must try to ensure that nothing bad ever happens.'

  We discuss breaking out of these limiting rules and beliefs in Chapter 7.

- **Strategies:** You develop strategies and responses to try to prevent anxiety occurring – for example, repeatedly checking that things are okay and avoiding things that make you feel anxious. But your attempts to prevent anxiety occurring only reinforce your view that anxiety is both bad and still uncontrollable. Head to Chapter 4 for pointers on putting yourself in situations you've been avoiding.

- **Stress:** If you're experiencing stress (for example, at work, at home or in relationships), you find it more difficult to exert control over your feelings of anxiety and to switch anxiety off.

- **Thought patterns:** You may develop ways of thinking about threats and challenges that just makes them seem worse rather than better. For example, you only think through all the bad things that could happen rather than thinking through how to resolve the problem. We look at understanding and dealing with catastrophic thinking in Chapter 6.

You can see that relatively few of these examples of how anxiety can come to feel uncontrollable relate to external events and experiences. Most relate to the way you think about the things that might be threats or challenges in your life and how you try to deal with them and the anxiety they cause.

Looking at types of anxiety problems

When anxiety becomes a problem, it can manifest itself in a number of specific and very different ways, each of which is distressing to the individual who suffers from the symptoms. We don't yet fully understand why some people develop one type of anxiety symptom rather than another, but these various symptoms form the basis for the main anxiety problems that people experience:

- **Chronic worrying:** Chronic, apparently uncontrollable worrying forms the basis for the diagnostic category known as *generalised anxiety disorder*. People who experience chronic worrying direct their worrying not only at major life issues (health, finances and so on) but also at many minor day-to-day issues that most people don't find problematic (a minor news item, a small mark on the carpet and so on). Chronic worrying is distressing because sufferers feel the need to worry, but find their worrying difficult to manage – they can't just turn it on and switch it off. They tend to catastrophise what they worry about, and end up turning even minor problems into major ones. We give guidance for dealing with chronic worry in Chapter 6.

- **Compulsions and rituals:** For some people, anxiety is associated with the need to indulge in compulsive or ritualistic behaviours that the individual believes will terminate or prevent anxiety. Common forms of compulsive behaviour include the following:

  - Compulsive checking, to ensure that bad things won't happen.

  - Compulsive washing/cleaning, to ensure that the person won't become contaminated or ill.

- Superstitious stereotyped sequences of behaviours – for example, touching the light switch ten times before switching it off.

- Superstitious arranging of objects – for example, making sure that ornaments on the mantelpiece are in their correct places.

Compulsions are distressing because people feel that they're compelled to do them, and they may become very distressed if they're prevented from enacting their compulsions and rituals when they feel they need to.

✔ **Obsessive thoughts:** Anxiety can cause intrusive and recurring thoughts about:

- Real future threats or challenges that the individual finds particularly aversive – for example, going to the dentist or sitting an exam.

- Thinking, doing or saying something that the person finds disturbing – for example, causing harm to a loved one or doing or saying something inappropriate and embarrassing.

✔ **Panic:** Some people experience anxiety in the form of regular, recurring *panic attacks* – intense and sudden periods of discomfort characterised by palpitations, sweating, trembling, dizziness and feelings of depersonalisation (feeling that you're outside of your body looking at yourself) and losing control. Panic attacks become a problem when they're very regular and disrupt people's ability to live their normal daily life. For the sufferer, these regular attacks are frightening and distressing.

✔ **Specific phobias:** Some people develop specific *phobias*: anxieties only around specific objects and events. Common examples of specific phobias are fears of small animals (such as spiders, insects, invertebrates, rodents and snakes), heights, water, blood and enclosed spaces (such as lifts). The anxiety caused by these fears is usually well out of proportion to the threat that these objects and situations pose, but the fears can result in distress and disruption of normal daily living if they become very severe. Flick to Chapter 4 for more information on dealing with severe fears.

Developing the Ability to Manage Your Anxiety

CBT is a proven, evidence-based way of helping you to alleviate your anxiety. The C stands for *cognitive*, which primarily relates to what you think, and the B stands for *behavioural*, which relates to what you do. CBT explains how what you think and do interacts with your feelings of anxiety to keep them going and make them worse. And, crucially, CBT provides ways of reducing anxiety through changing what you think and do.

Exploring the role of anxious thoughts

Try the following activity that explores the role of thinking in relation to anxiety. If it helps, you may want to close your eyes (but only after you've read this activity first!).

Imagine that you're visiting a doctor because you're experiencing an unexplained pain in your foot. You respect and trust this doctor and know that she'll take her time to reach the correct diagnosis. After a series of tests, she tells you that you've no reason to be concerned; you don't have a serious illness. Rather, she explains, you've a bruised tendon that will begin to heal within the next week or so, provided you don't overexert yourself. How do you feel at the end of this consultation?

Now repeat the process of imagining visiting a doctor because of foot pain. The level and location of the pain is identical to that in the previous scenario, and your trusted doctor runs the same tests. This time, however, the news isn't so good. The doctor returns looking worried. She explains that she isn't yet sure what's wrong, but is concerned enough to urgently refer you to a specialist for further tests. How do you feel at the end of this consultation?

Probably, you imagined feeling relieved at the end of the first scenario and anxious at the end of the second. Given that the pain is the same in both cases, what leads to the different feelings?

Well, the different reactions of the doctor mean that you're likely to *think* differently about the pain in the two scenarios. In the first you may have thoughts like 'the pain isn't serious', which lead you to feel relieved. In the second you probably have more fearful thoughts, such as 'something may be seriously wrong with me', which lead you to feel anxious.

A key principle of CBT is that thoughts affect how you feel, and fearful or worrying thoughts can lead you to feel anxious.

Sometimes, your fearful thoughts are realistic. However, more often than not, your fearful thoughts don't accurately reflect the reality of the situation. Rather, the thoughts:

- ✔ Overestimate the likelihood of the feared outcome.
- ✔ Overestimate the awfulness of the feared outcome.
- ✔ Underestimate your ability to cope if the feared outcome happens.

For example, if you're anxious about making a mistake at work, you may:

- ✔ Think that you're very likely to make a mistake, when in fact you usually don't make them.
- ✔ Think that the consequence of a mistake would be losing your job, when in fact this loss is very unlikely.
- ✔ Think that you wouldn't be able to cope if you made a mistake, when in fact you'd probably manage the situation well and correct the error.

In this book we use the phrase 'coping with the feared outcome' to refer to your ability to successfully manage things should your fears come to pass.

Unrealistic fears occur because of the second principle of CBT: feelings bias your thinking, and feelings of anxiety can lead you to have more fearful thoughts and to pay attention to more anxiety-provoking things.

If you're not immediately convinced by this second principle, try to recall two times when you thought about the same issue, once when you were feeling calm and once when you were feeling anxious. Then take a few moments to reflect on any differences between what you thought about the issue in the two cases. The chances are that you had more fearful and worrying thoughts about the issue when you were feeling anxious than when you were feeling calm. Feelings biased your thinking.

The combination of the two principles means a circular relationship can develop between fearful thoughts and anxious feelings, as illustrated in Figure 1-1. Unfortunately, you can get stuck in a vicious cycle of increasing fear and anxiety.

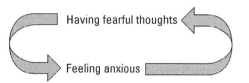

Having fearful thoughts

Feeling anxious

Figure 1-1: The relationship between fearful thoughts and anxious feelings.

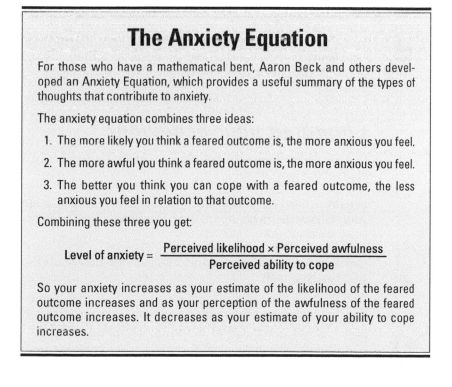

The Anxiety Equation

For those who have a mathematical bent, Aaron Beck and others developed an Anxiety Equation, which provides a useful summary of the types of thoughts that contribute to anxiety.

The anxiety equation combines three ideas:

1. The more likely you think a feared outcome is, the more anxious you feel.

2. The more awful you think a feared outcome is, the more anxious you feel.

3. The better you think you can cope with a feared outcome, the less anxious you feel in relation to that outcome.

Combining these three you get:

$$\text{Level of anxiety} = \frac{\text{Perceived likelihood} \times \text{Perceived awfulness}}{\text{Perceived ability to cope}}$$

So your anxiety increases as your estimate of the likelihood of the feared outcome increases and as your perception of the awfulness of the feared outcome increases. It decreases as your estimate of your ability to cope increases.

If you're someone who tends to visualise things, you may experience some anxious thoughts in the form of mental images. For example, you may see a mental image of what you fear will go wrong. As with other types of anxious thoughts, images can increase feelings of anxiety, which in turn can lead to more anxiety-related images and thoughts.

Given that anxious thoughts often contribute to your anxiety by exaggerating the risks you face, one way that CBT can help reduce anxiety is through re-evaluating these thoughts. In the following chapters we explain a range of CBT techniques that help you re-evaluate your anxious thoughts and replace them with more realistic and helpful ones.

In essence, the CBT techniques help you to identify when your anxious thoughts are exaggerating the level of risk, and to develop more helpful thoughts that provide a more realistic assessment of the risk. These new thoughts are most likely to be less anxiety provoking, leading to a reduction in your level of anxiety.

When reading about and applying CBT techniques, don't blame or criticise yourself for having anxious thoughts that exaggerate the level of risk. Everyone has such thoughts when they feel anxious or stressed – having them is a normal human process.

Changing your behaviour

Understanding how your behaviour contributes to anxiety is of crucial importance.

Usually, when you feel anxious, you do things to try to keep yourself, and perhaps others, safe. Examples of such *safety behaviours* include:

- ✔ Regularly visiting a doctor, if you're continually worried that you're ill.
- ✔ Rushing through a presentation you're giving in order to finish it quicker, in the belief that rushing reduces the chances of you making a highly embarrassing mistake.
- ✔ Sitting or lying down when you feel your heart racing, in the hope that doing so puts less strain on your body and so means that you don't suffer the heart attack you fear.

Safety behaviours also include avoiding the anxiety-provoking situation altogether. Here are some examples of avoidance:

✔ Not leaving the house, if you fear you'll be laughed at and humiliated by others if you do.

✔ Not driving a car, if you think that a car crash is likely.

✔ Not using lifts, if you're afraid you'll become trapped in one.

Sometimes avoidance can mean that you rarely feel anxious, because you're so infrequently in the feared situation. However, avoidance is far from an ideal solution, because it can severely limit your life and may not always be possible.

Although safety behaviours (including avoidance) are a normal and understandable response to anxiety, they can maintain and worsen anxiety problems. Safety behaviours can prevent you from engaging in new learning about the things you fear.

Craig strongly believes that he'll be attacked if he leaves his home, so he stays at home day after day after day. Because Craig avoids leaving his home, he never has an opportunity to see whether his perception of the risk is accurate or excessive. And so the fear remains.

In contrast, if you *don't* engage in safety behaviours, several things can happen:

✔ Because fears tend to significantly exaggerate the level of risk, you may find that the feared outcome doesn't come to pass or, if it does, that it's much less awful than you imagined.

✔ Feelings of anxiety gradually diminish as you remain in the feared situation, because the level of danger is lower.

✔ You realise that your anxious thoughts have exaggerated the level of risk. This realisation reduces your strength of belief in these thoughts and provides convincing evidence for the development of more realistic thoughts. And this shift in thinking helps you feel less anxious.

CBT reduces anxiety by supporting you to face what you fear without safety behaviours.

At this point you may be thinking that CBT isn't for you, and the prospect of facing your fears may seem impossible or dangerous. Don't worry. The CBT techniques we describe in the following chapters help you assess whether your estimate of the level of risk is exaggerated and so whether facing your fears is likely to be safe. And you can manage the process of facing your fears in a gradual way that's under your control.

Chapter 2

Making a Map of Your Anxiety

In This Chapter

▶ Focusing on an experience that makes you anxious

▶ Thinking about triggers, images, bodily sensations and actions

▶ Developing a map of your anxiety that explains what keeps it going

*W*hen you set out on a new journey, taking a map is helpful. The map gives you a sense of the terrain you're heading into and you can use it to help plan your route. The map also helps you to make decisions about route changes if you meet an unexpected obstacle.

Similarly, creating a map of your anxiety before you embark on your journey of recovery is useful. This chapter guides you through the creation process. We help you apply your general understanding of anxiety to your specific difficulties, and by the end of the chapter you have a map that explains what maintains your anxiety from a CBT perspective. Subsequent chapters use this map to help you plan your journey of recovery from anxiety.

Putting Your Anxiety Under the Microscope

You need to place your anxiety under the microscope and examine its key features:

- Situations and events that can trigger your anxiety.
- Thoughts and images that you experience when anxious.
- Bodily sensations that accompany your anxiety.
- Things that you do (or don't do) when anxious or to avoid anxiety.

These features form the building blocks of the map. The map shows how these elements interact to maintain and worsen your anxiety, and contains a list of your strengths and resources that can help in the journey ahead.

What if I'm anxious about examining my anxiety?

Sometimes the prospect of thinking about your anxiety and examining its features can be anxiety-provoking in itself. This feeling is normal and understandable. If you're not feeling anxiety in relation to examining your anxiety, that's great – you can stop reading this sidebar now and return to the main chapter. If your anxiety is relatively mild then say to yourself, 'This is something I need to do to help myself and it'll be worth it,' and then also continue with the chapter.

If, however, your fear of examining anxiety is more intense, we suggest that you tackle this specific fear first. Continue with this chapter, using your fear of examining anxiety as the only specific example to develop the map. Then turn to Part II of this book and work through all of its chapters in order, applying the approaches we describe there to this specific fear. After you reduce this fear, you can then revisit the current chapter and develop a map of your anxiety more generally and work through the rest of the book again in relation to your other fears.

Finally, if none of the above work for you, remember that other sources of help are available in relation to overcoming anxiety. Visiting your family doctor for advice and perhaps a referral for face-to-face therapy is a good place to start.

Picking a specific example

To begin the mapping process, you need a specific example of anxiety to focus your 'microscope' upon. You can start with a recent occurrence of anxiety that's fresh in your memory.

Grab a pen and paper and make a list of times you can remember that you've been anxious over the past two weeks. Now pick one example from this list to focus on for the rest of this chapter. If possible, choose an example that you remember well and that's relatively typical of the anxiety that you experience. If you can't decide, or if no example quite fits the bill, just pick the example that's clearest in your memory. Later on, you have the chance to repeat the mapping process for other examples.

Identifying triggers for anxiety

The first feature of anxiety that you need for the map is its trigger or triggers.

Call the example that you've chosen to mind and 'rewind' the memory as best you can to the events that preceded the anxiety. Did something happen, or did you think that something might happen, to trigger the anxiety? Here are a few examples of possible triggers:

- ✔ **Something occurring that you fear:** For example, a spider appearing, the telephone ringing, your heart missing a beat or a distressing thought coming to mind.

- ✔ **Anticipating needing to do something that you fear:** For example, anticipating leaving the house, speaking to a group of people or travelling by car.

- ✔ **Finding yourself in a situation that you fear:** For example, becoming caught up in a crowd or meeting someone you're scared of by chance.

- ✔ **Being faced with an uncertain situation that you can't resolve right now:** For example, awaiting the results of medical tests or a job interview.

If you're clear what the trigger(s) were, note them down. You can use a record sheet like that in Table 2-1. If you remain unsure about the triggers, perhaps talk through the example with a friend or family member and ask what he or she thinks triggered your anxiety.

Table 2-1	Example Record Sheet
Behaviours	
Bodily Sensations	
Thoughts and Images	
Situation/Triggers	

Many people judge themselves harshly and think that they're feeble or pathetic because they're afraid of something that other people aren't. If this self-judgement is what you tend to do, be as kind and gentle with yourself as possible. Call to mind a good friend or caring relative and think about what he or she might say in response to your self-criticism.

Sometimes neither you nor a friend or relative can identify what's made you anxious, because at times the triggers for anxiety can be quite hard to spot. Don't worry if that's the case. The anxiety diary we introduce in the later section 'Elaborating on the map' collects more information that can help.

Spotting anxious thoughts and images

If possible, you need to determine the key thoughts, and perhaps also images, that went through your mind when you were anxious.

Call your example back to mind and ask yourself: 'What was going through my mind when I was anxious?' Then move on to the following questions about your experiences *at that time*:

- ✔ What did you fear would happen?

- ✔ What was the worst-case scenario that you imagined?

- ✔ At the time, how likely did it seem that the worst-case would occur? (If you like numbers, you can rate this worst-case on a 0 to 100 scale, with 0 being 'not going to happen' and 100 being 'a dead certainty it would'.)

- ✔ How well or badly did you think that you would be able to cope if the worst-case happened?

- ✔ Did you have any anxiety-provoking images in your mind (for example, a picture of the worst-case scenario)? Note that not everyone experiences anxious images.

Keep a note of your answers to these questions on your record sheet. You need them in the later section 'Drawing the Map'.

If you're struggling to answer the questions, don't worry; an example can help. Imagine that you're afraid of flying, and you're sitting on an aeroplane waiting for take-off. You may answer the questions like this:

- ✔ Fear: 'It's going to crash!'

- ✔ Worst-case: 'I'll die and it'll be painful.'

- ✔ Estimated likelihood: 90 out of 100.

- ✔ Ability to cope: 'I'm trapped and can't do anything.'

- ✔ Image: The plane crashing into the sea.

Revisiting the anxiety equation

This sidebar is for those of you who have a mathematical bent. If you find maths challenging, the following is unlikely to be helpful – go ahead and skip it.

The anxiety equation states that:

Level of anxiety = Perceived likelihood of worst case × Perceived awfulness of worst case ÷ Perceived ability to cope

So in the fear of flying example, the equation reads as follows:

High anxiety =

High perceived likelihood (90 per cent) × **High** perceived awfulness (painful death)

÷ **Low** perceived ability to cope ('I'm trapped and can't do anything')

Try writing an anxiety equation that captures your fears by circulating the levels that best fit for you:

Anxiety: Low/Medium/High =

Likelihood: Low/Medium/High × Awfulness: Low/Medium/High

÷ Ability to cope: High/Medium/Low

For an introduction to the anxiety equation, head to Chapter 1.

Hopefully, this example gives more of a concrete sense of what you're looking for here. However, if you continue to struggle to answer these questions, don't worry. Sometimes you're not aware of the fears connected with your anxiety, especially if you often avoid anxiety-provoking situations. The anxiety diary, described in the later section 'Elaborating on the Map', can help.

How was my body feeling?

Bodily sensations can be another key feature of anxiety.

Call to mind the memory of your chosen example and see whether you can remember what bodily sensations you were experiencing at that time. For example, you may have felt:

- ✔ A headache
- ✔ Hot or cold flushes or sweating
- ✔ Lightheaded or dizzy
- ✔ Nauseous
- ✔ Physical tension, sometimes to a painful level
- ✔ Racing or pounding heart or chest pain
- ✔ Shivers and shakes
- ✔ Shortness of breath or difficulty breathing

Note down any sensations on your record sheet. Don't worry if you don't remember. Sometimes you can be so caught up in your fears, you don't notice what's happening in your body.

All of the above bodily sensations can be a symptom of high anxiety. However, particularly if chest pain or breathing problems are part of your experience, check with your doctor that these problems are due to anxiety and not some other medical condition before applying the techniques in this book.

Many of the body sensations associated with anxiety can be intense and frightening. But they can be a normal feature of anxiety and occur as a result of the evolutionary fight, flight and freeze responses to danger.

What did I do (or not do)?

What you do in response to anxiety can play a crucial role in maintaining and sometimes worsening it. Therefore, you need to closely examine your anxiety-related behaviour.

With your chosen example in mind, ask yourself the following:

- ✔ What did I do in response to my anxiety and fear?
- ✔ How did I try to keep myself safe?
- ✔ Did I do anything that I thought may have prevented the worst case from occurring?
- ✔ Do I avoid anything in life because of this specific fear and anxiety?

When answering these questions, remember that behaviour can be something you do *externally*, like walking away from a scary situation, or *internally*, like counting in your head to try to stop thinking about something anxiety provoking. As previously, note down your answers for use later.

If you're struggling, the following examples of anxiety-related behaviour can help:

- ✔ Avoiding things that you fear (for example not going out).
- ✔ Trying to ensure that you have an escape route from anxiety-provoking situations and using this route when needed.
- ✔ Seeking reassurance and support from friends or relatives (for example only leaving the house in someone else's company).
- ✔ Repeatedly checking something for reassurance.
- ✔ Trying to distract yourself from worry, or trying to suppress it.
- ✔ Dwelling on a fear or worry to try to resolve it.

You may also find asking friends or family members what you do in response to anxiety helpful.

Drawing Your Map

The previous section helps you write down some of the key features of your anxiety example. Now you need to combine the features to make your map.

Adding the features

Figure 2-1 provides a template for your anxiety map.

To create the map, first copy the template in Figure 2-1 onto a larger sheet of paper. If you have access to a photocopier, use that to enlarge the image. Then fill in the various sections with the features that you identified, to get a good picture of the terrain.

Figure 2-2 gives an example of a completed map, so you know the sort of thing that you're aiming for. This map shows one situation. You may want to include more examples in yours, or draw different maps for different anxieties.

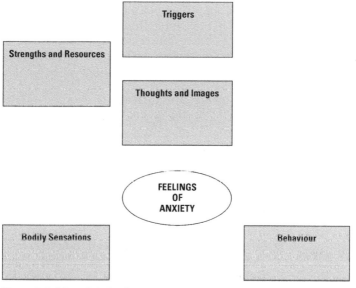

Figure 2-1: A template for the map.

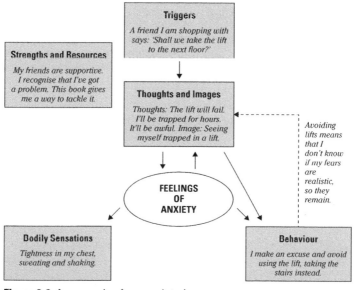

Figure 2-2: An example of a completed map.

Linking the features

The map contains five features: triggers, thoughts and images, bodily sensations, behaviours, and the feelings of anxiety. You need to add in the connections between these five features, because these connections explain what maintains your anxiety. The map contains dotted arrows that indicate common connections between the features.

Consider each arrow in turn and answer the following questions:

✔ Do your triggers tend to lead to anxious thoughts or images? If they do, thicken the arrow leading from 'triggers' to 'thoughts and images'.

✔ Do your thoughts or images tend to make you feel more anxious? If so, thicken the arrow leading from 'thoughts and images' to 'feelings of anxiety'.

✔ Do your feelings of anxiety lead to further or stronger thoughts/images? If so, thicken the arrow leading from 'feelings of anxiety' to 'thoughts and images'.

✔ Do your feelings of anxiety lead to bodily sensations? If so, thicken the arrow leading from 'feelings of anxiety' to 'bodily sensations'.

✔ Do you have anxious thoughts or worries about the bodily sensations (for example, a pounding heart leading to fears about having a heart attack)? If so, add an arrow leading from 'bodily sensations' to 'thoughts and images'.

✔ Do anxious thoughts, images or feelings lead you to do (or avoid doing) anything, in the hope that this will keep you safe and reduce anxiety? If so, thicken the relevant arrows leading to 'behaviours'.

✔ Do the behaviours prevent you from discovering whether your fears are realistic or excessive? If so, add arrows leadings from 'behaviours' to 'feelings of anxiety' and to 'thoughts and images'.

Don't worry if you're not sure about the answers to some of these questions. Have another look at the example in Figure 2-2 and then just do the best you can. Part II of this book covers these issues in more detail.

Elaborating on the map

Now that you have a map of an example of your anxiety, you can repeat the process for other recent examples. You then have a more complete picture of the anxiety you experience and a firmer foundation and useful resource for subsequent chapters.

Choose another example from your list, go to 'Identifying triggers for anxiety' earlier in this chapter, and repeat all the steps from there onwards. When you come to create the map of this new example, if its features are similar to the previous example, add them to the existing map. If they're quite different, however, draw a new map. Keep repeating this process until you've mapped examples of all the types of anxiety that you typically experience and want to work on. You may end up with several maps.

If your map or maps have important gaps in them, for example sparse thoughts and images sections, you need to collect more information about your anxiety's features. A good way of doing so is to keep an anxiety diary, using Table 2-2 as a model.

Table 2-2		Anxiety Diary			
Date and Time	Situation/ Triggers	Feelings	Thoughts and Images	Bodily Sensations	Behaviours
Monday 11 a.m.	A friend I'm shopping with says: 'Shall we take the lift to the next floor?'	Anxiety	Thoughts: The lift will fail. I'll be trapped for hours. It'll be awful. Image: Seeing myself trapped in a lift.	Tightness in my chest, sweating and shaking	I make an excuse and avoid using the lift, taking the stairs instead.

Do your best to complete your diary every time you feel anxious, over a period of a week. Try to follow the same format as in Table 2-2. After the week has passed, review the contents of the diary to see whether you've discovered any new features to add to the map(s). Usually, the diary highlights new aspects of your anxiety, because you're paying closer attention to your anxiety and don't have to rely on memory.

Including your strengths and resources

So far the map(s) you've developed is/are solely problem-focused. The finishing touch (at least for now!) is to add a list of the strengths and resources that you can draw on in your journey ahead.

Making a list of strengths and resources isn't always easy, because you can often discount your abilities and sources of support. However, start this process by asking yourself: 'What am I good at?' and 'What sources of support can I draw on?' Also seek the views of friends and family about this. The following examples of strengths and resources may help generate ideas:

- ✔ Awareness of the features of your anxiety.

- ✔ Family and friends.

- ✔ Motivation to change (after all, you're motivated enough to read this chapter).

- ✔ This book (!).

Using Your Map

So how can you best use your map to help reduce anxiety? Part II of this book looks at how you can reduce anxiety in detail, but briefly you have two main ways:

- ✔ **Thinking differently:** Your map illustrates the crucial contribution that thoughts and images can make to feelings of anxiety. It may also show how anxiety can lead these thoughts and images to grow in strength. Anxious thoughts and images often make things seem a lot worse than they really are.

  In Part II you find ways of testing out your thoughts to see whether they're realistic. You also discover ways of developing, and believing, more helpful thoughts that are less anxiety provoking.

- ✔ **Doing things that help:** Your map shows the effect that doing things (or not doing things) has on your anxiety.

For example, avoiding the things you fear may have helped the fear to grow.

Part II describes how you can face fears in a gradual and safe way. Often, facing fears can reduce anxiety because your fears usually won't come to pass.

If you read through Part II of this book but find that the techniques described don't help with your anxiety, or if the idea of trying them feels too overwhelming, don't worry. Self-help books such as this one aren't the best approach for everyone. Instead, visit your doctor and ask what other forms of therapy are available to you. For example, the doctor may be able to refer you to see a cognitive-behavioural psychotherapist who can work with you to help overcome your anxiety. The map that you've drawn may be a helpful starting point for your work together.

Part II
Tackling Your Anxiety

The 5th Wave   By Rich Tennant

"Dora's anxiety has always manifested itself in the 'flight response.'"

In this part . . .

We give you a toolkit of tried and tested methods to start to overcome your anxiety. We guide you through ways of facing your fears, testing out if the worst case scenario is really true, letting go of worries and not being ruled by perfectionism or taking too much responsibility. Pick the chapters that best fit the difficulties you're experiencing, or work through each chapter in turn.

Chapter 3

Going for Goals

In This Chapter

▶ Being clear on what you want to achieve

▶ Maximising your chances of success with SMART goals

▶ Taking one step at a time

▶ Putting your map and goals together so you know what to do next

*E*veryone needs goals in life, and people have different types of goals depending on what they're doing at the time – practical goals such as being able to get to a destination for a certain time, or lifestyle goals such as getting fit or losing weight. Unless you have these targets that you aim for, your direction is unclear.

Say you're going on a train journey. You need to know where you're going and when, and on the train you look out of the window for landmarks that let you know where you are and how much further you have to go. You need a place to start and a place to end to anchor the journey in the middle and help you stay on track and not wander off the course.

Understanding the nature and the workings of your anxieties is the start of your journey. Your goals represent the end of the journey. This chapter helps you think about where you want to end up, helping you to plan so that you achieve your aspirations.

Planning Your Goals

When planning your goals, start by thinking about what you don't want in your life anymore and what you'd like to be in your life that isn't there now.

Perhaps you've a sense of how you'd like things to be, but have difficulty putting it into words, or you're clear about how you *don't* want to feel but don't feel so confident as to what your life would look like if you didn't feel as you do at the moment. You may have got fed up with feeling the way you do or you may have a specific reason for dealing with your anxiety.

Make sure that your goals about overcoming your anxiety are your own – things you want to achieve for yourself, rather than what others may want you to achieve. You're far more likely to achieve something that's important to you.

If I was to wake up one day without anxiety . . .

Think about this idea. How would your life be if you didn't feel anxious? Would you feel calm? Happy? Chilled out?

If we met you leading your life in this calm, relaxed way, what would you be doing that would be different from now; what might we see?

If we then ask you what kind of thoughts were going through your mind, you start to build up a picture of how you would like things to be for you and can start to clarify your goal of reducing your anxiety.

Measuring anxiety

How would you know that your anxiety was less or even gone? Consider how you feel when you're anxious. What thoughts go through your mind? How does your body feel, for example?

One of the ways you can think about how anxious you feel is to use a measure. The anxiety score is a simple 0–10 scale where 0 means no anxiety and 10 means as much anxiety as you can bear, with measures in the middle showing your increasing level of discomfort. You can use this anxiety score to help measure your goal of lessening your anxiety.

Thinking about others' involvement

People rarely live in isolation. Most have friends and families, partners and children around them who are often aware of anxieties and develop ways to support their loved one. People who care for you often compensate for your anxieties. They might do things for you, manage things you're fearful of, check things for you and reassure you.

Think about what others would see if your anxiety was to go. Would you be less likely to ask them for help or reassurance? Would you rely on them less, or maybe do more with them?

You may measure the success of your goal based on how much or how little you involve others in your anxiety difficulties.

Anxiety can have an unhelpful effect on relationships, but you need people around to support you through overcoming your difficulties. You may not have told people close to you that you're anxious, or, conversely, you may be asking too much of people in helping you. Having people to support you is important, but so is standing on our own two feet. Sometimes, relying on others for help with your anxiety can keep the anxiety going.

Making Goals SMART

In order to maximise the chances of succeeding with your goals for managing your anxiety, you need to make it SMART – specific, measurable, achievable, realistic, and time-orientated. This section shows you how.

Perhaps you have one goal or more than one goal in mind – that's okay, but don't have too many. Working on more than one goal at a time can make things more difficult and you want the journey to be manageable. See the later section 'Hopping Across the Stepping Stones to Success' for more information on this issue.

Defining SMART

If your vision is too vague, your hard work can go off track. To help you organise your goals in a way that makes you more likely to achieve them, make them SMART:

- ✔ **Specific:** What exactly do I want to achieve, when and where do I want to achieve it, does anyone else need to be involved and what would be the purpose or benefit of achieving this goal?

- ✔ **Measurable.** How will I know when I've accomplished this goal? What will I be doing, and how will I be thinking and feeling?

- ✔ **Achievable.** Is it feasible and within my reach to attain this goal?

- ✔ **Realistic.** Have I got the skills, motivation and willingness to achieve this goal?

- ✔ **Time orientated.** By when do I want to achieve this goal? What are realistic time frames?

SMARTing up your goal

Look at the goal you've set yourself. Is it SMART? What do you need to do to make it SMART? Take a look at the goal below:

> **Goal:** To get over my fear of spiders

Ask yourself: Is this goal specific? What do I mean by 'getting over my fear'? How would I know? By when would I like to have achieved my goal?

A SMARTer goal is:

> **SMARTer Goal:** To stay in a room with a spider long enough to scoop it up into a dustpan and put it outside on

at least three occasions within the next eight weeks with an anxiety score of no more than 3.

This goal is smarter because the goal is:

✔ **Specific:** You know exactly what you're trying to achieve.

✔ **Measurable.** You can measure success with the anxiety score (see 'Measuring anxiety', earlier in the chapter).

✔ **Achievable.** You feel that achieving this goal is reasonable.

✔ **Realistic.** You feel that you can do this.

✔ **Time orientated.** You have eight weeks in which to achieve the goal.

Table 3-1 shows examples of anxious people, their vague goals and how those goals transform into SMART ones.

Table 3-1 Examples of Making Goals SMART

Person	Anxiety	Vague Goal	SMART Goal
Gill	Eating in social situations	To eat out without feeling anxious	To eat lunch at the Italian restaurant in the high street with Susan and Peter on at least three occasions within the next eight weeks with an anxiety score of no more than 2
Peter	Driving in traffic	To drive without feeling anxious	To drive from my house into the town six miles away and back again in the middle of the day on my own on at least four occasions within the next eight weeks with an anxiety score of no more than 2
Tony	Leaving the front door unlocked when he goes out to work	To go to work and not think about my front door being locked	To lock my front door once, get in the car and go to work without retuning to check the door until I open it again at the end of the day for five days in a row within the next ten weeks with an anxiety score of no more than 2

These goals all have SMART ingredients. They're specific about what Gill, Peter and Tony want to achieve. They can measure success by the use of anxiety scores, and the goals are realistic and achievable for most people who want to just be able to manage their fear successfully within a time allocation.

You know what's realistic for you to be able to change within the time you've decided. Use the SMART Goal Form in Figure 3-1 to map out your goal.

Write down your long term and interim SMART goals here. Remember they need to be **S**pecific, **M**easurable, **A**chievable, **R**ealistic and **T**ime orientated.	
SMART goal:	
I hope to achieve this goal by this date:	
Interim SMART goal 1:	To be achieved by this date:
Interim SMART goal 2:	To be achieved by this date:
Interim SMART goal 3:	To be achieved by this date:

Figure 3-1: SMART Goal Form. _____

Making the goal achievable

You may have had enough of your anxiety and feel that now's the time to start tackling it. Or perhaps you want to launch yourself into activities that you've previously been afraid to do. Or you may have an event coming up soon that you'd like to be able to attend but at present your anxiety is getting in the way.

To make a goal that has every chance of success, think about the practical considerations:

- ✔ Do you need any help from others around you?

- ✔ How can you plan your time in order to stand the best chance of succeeding?

- ✔ Do you have the opportunity to practise the steps that will lead to achievement of your goal?

- ✔ Are there any other situations you need to deal with before you tackle this task? For example, do you have any other worries at the moment that are playing on your mind such as an unpaid bill, or other practical things that need sorting out? If you do, get these practical problems solved first so you can concentrate on your SMART goal.

Make sure that you have any help you need available to you. Take a look at the examples in Table 3-1. If Gill wants to practise eating out with Susan and Peter, she needs to make sure that they're available. Tony needs the agreement of anyone he lives with to make sure that he's the last one to leave the house. Peter may need to take a couple of days off in the week to practise driving in the middle of the day.

You may also want to talk with others supporting you about how long overcoming this anxiety may take. Your friends and family will find it useful to know that it may take you a while to achieve your goals and that you need their support throughout a process that may take several weeks or even months.

Hopping Across the Stepping Stones to Success

Now that you know your SMART goal, think about the best way to succeed. What you need to do is take your time, break the task down and get support.

Taking your time

If you try to attempt to achieve your goal all at once, you might fail – after all, if you could just do what it is that you want to achieve then you'd have probably done it already.

You might feel as if you're raring to go and want to get stuck in straight away. Imagine that you decide you're just going to face your fear and be done with it. Although tackling the anxiety head on might work in the short term, you may not get rid of the anxiety in the longer term. When it comes to learning new skills, one step at a time ensures that the change stays with you, incorporated successfully into your life.

Think of a skill you learned sometime in your life. It might be a skill from childhood such as riding a bike, swimming or playing a musical instrument, or a skill you learned as an adult, such as driving a car. Consider the journey you went on, or are maybe still continuing. Make a list of the elements you needed that enabled you to succeed. Your list might include things like practice, doing it with a friend and being prepared for it to take a long time. Now think about how many of those elements apply to achieving your present goal, and recognise that learning the skill took time.

Breaking down the task

Achieving a goal can feel like a huge task, even if you think that the goal is realistic and achievable. Breaking the journey to the goal down into manageable, bite-sized chunks makes a daunting task seem easier.

For example, if you're trying to lose weight, you might have a target weight in mind, but you also have some interim goals.

Your overall goal might be to lose one stone, but you set interim goals of two pounds per week.

Take the example of Peter, who finds it difficult to drive in traffic. Here's his overall SMART goal:

> To drive from my house into the town six miles away and back again in the middle of the day on my own on at least four occasions within the next eight weeks with an anxiety score of no more than 2.

Peter has eight weeks in which to achieve this goal, which feels like a long time, so he needs to set interim goals. Peter can divide the interim goals into distances, quieter and more crowded places and perhaps those with varying speed limits. So his interim goals can be as follows:

- ✔ **By the end of Week 2:** To drive for five minutes in the roads around my house on at least five occasions.

- ✔ **By the end of Week 4:** To drive to my friend's house ten minutes away through the centre of the village and then drive back again using the same route on at least five occasions.

- ✔ **By the end of Week 6:** To join the dual carriageway at junction x and stay on until junction y while maintaining a speed similar to other road users, on at least five occasions.

These interim goals then leave the final two weeks to practise driving into the town until Peter has achieved his goal of four occasions.

Now you have your SMART goal and have thought about making it achievable, try breaking your goal down into interim goals and decide how they fit into your day or week. Update your SMART Goal Form in Figure 3-1.

Enlisting support

Taking on the challenge of overcoming a fear or anxiety that you've had for some time takes hard work and courage. You may feel like you've a big mountain to climb, and sometimes you feel like giving up. At times like this, have someone there to support you – to let you know when you've done well and to encourage you to continue when you feel like you might give up. Think about a friend or family member who might be willing to support you with this change.

Susan decided that she wanted to overcome her fear of travelling on trains. She told her friend Ruth about this fear and how she had avoided travelling on trains for years. Ruth didn't realise that Susan had this problem, because Susan had always avoided the subject by suggesting that they would drive. When Susan finally told Ruth, she felt relieved and Ruth agreed to help Susan out. Susan explained that although she was going to do her best, she might need support. Ruth had recently started to go to the gym and was struggling to get the motivation to go, so Susan agreed that she would go to the gym with Ruth, and Ruth agreed to support Susan with overcoming her fear.

Map, Goal, Action!

Now it's time to take action! But where should you start? That depends on what's keeping your anxiety going (which you map out in Chapter 2) and on what your goals are.

In this book we concentrate on four main patterns that can keep anxiety going. You may recognise your own situation in just one of these patterns or, more likely, in several or all of them. These patterns correspond to the next four chapters.

So, if your map highlights that one of these patterns is particularly significant, and if your goals mean that you want to overcome this problem, head to the relevant chapter. We suggest that you follow the chapters in order if several apply to you, but you can go straight to one of the chapters if only that one seems relevant.

Avoiding people, places or things

Does your map particularly highlight avoidance of certain situations as something that keeps anxiety going for you? Avoidance is a factor that keeps most anxiety problems going, so Chapter 4 can be useful for a lot of different sorts of anxiety problem.

In Chapter 4 we show you how to face your fears step by step. Start here if you've a phobia of something specific, like spiders or seeing blood. We describe the simplest approach to tackling anxiety, so if you feel a bit overwhelmed already, head straight to Chapter 4.

Fearing the worst-case scenario coming true

Most anxiety problems persist because of fears of the worst happening. If this fear is a big feature in your map of anxiety, Chapter 5 can be particularly helpful. We help you check your fears against the facts to see whether they're realistic.

Chapter 5 is particularly important if you're anxious about panic attacks, social situations or any number of bad things happening. In fact, this chapter is useful for most anxiety problems.

Chewing over worries without finding a solution

Everyone worries sometimes, but some people get particularly stuck with worrying about a range of different topics, and find it hard to solve problems and let go of worry. Either way, if worrying less is important to achieving your goals, Chapter 6 is useful. If you can see that you're stuck in a pattern of worry, this chapter helps you break free.

Following troublesome rules

Some anxiety problems can hit you just because a bit of bad luck throws you off course. Others may be more likely to happen if you set particular troublesome rules for living your life. Common troublesome rules include thinking that you have to do everything perfectly, or that you're entirely responsible for things. Breaking these rules is unavoidable, but likely to be a source of anxiety.

Sticking with the journey

Understand that setbacks are normal and can even be helpful. Research shows that people who have setbacks while they're using CBT methods are more likely to stay recovered for good. This success happens because they learn from the setbacks. Top sportsmen and sportswomen say that the matches they lose teach them the most.

And at all times, remember why you want to make changes. Taking action to achieve your goals can be frightening and hard work. Sometimes you may feel like you want to give up. Remember the advantages of change, and weigh these against the disadvantages. The journey is worthwhile!

If you suspect that troublesome rules underlie your anxiety difficulties then Chapter 7 is for you. But still use the other chapters first if they apply to you. You can tackle the current problems and then come to this chapter if anxiety rules are slowing progress, or to stop them tripping you up in the future.

Chapter 4

Facing Your Fears

· ·

In This Chapter

▶ Seeing how fear affects you

▶ Breaking down your fears

▶ Overcoming fears, step by step

▶ Braving needles and blood

· ·

Some fears are quite common, such as a fear of spiders, mice, dogs, heights, confined spaces, flying and thunder and lightning. Others fears are a bit more unusual, such as a fear of buttons or cotton wool. Whatever your fear is, the process for diminishing it is the same.

This chapter helps you understand how your fears work, reminds you that avoidance can feed fears (refer to Chapter 1), and gives you a systematic way to move past your fears.

Facing things that scare you can feel like a daunting task. Although it takes a degree of courage, facing your fears step by step means that with a little determination you can reduce your fear and the impact it has on your life.

At some time or another everyone does things that make them feel anxious or scared, but after you take the plunge and try something you'd rather have not done, you may find that the experience wasn't as bad as you expected.

Knowing How Fear Works

Think about your biggest fear. What thoughts and images go through your mind in relation to this fear? What happens in your body in relation to these thoughts and images? How do you react?

The fight, flight and freeze response is an evolutionary survival response that helps keep you safe. Your body recognises danger and reacts accordingly to make you physically primed to do one of the following:

- ✔ Defend yourself.

- ✔ Get away quickly.

- ✔ Assume a state that draws as little attention as possible in the hope that the threat passes you by.

When you're frightened, the body releases chemicals such as adrenaline, noradrenalin and cortisol that create changes in the body. The following list outlines some of the main physical changes that being afraid creates, and why the body reacts as it does. As you read, think about how many of these physical symptoms apply to you when you're anxious. However, if you're afraid of blood or needles, you may have a different reaction (see the later section 'Tackling a fear of blood or needles').

- ✔ **Your vision improves.** Your pupils open out so you can see more clearly, even in the dark.

- ✔ **The hairs on your body stand on end.** You're more sensitive to your environment and (theoretically) appear larger, to hopefully intimidate your opponent.

- ✔ **Your heart pounds.** Your heart rate increases so the main organs and muscles can work harder.

- ✔ **You breathe faster.** Your lungs, throat and nostrils open up so that you get extra oxygen to allow your system to work harder and faster. Deeper breathing also helps you to shout or scream more loudly!

✔ **Your mouth goes dry and you need to go to the toilet.**
Fatty cells are activated to create instant energy and sys-
tems that aren't essential, such as the digestive system,
shut down. So your mouth has less saliva, and the bowels
and bladder may open out. The toilet urge may also make
you feel lighter and therefore more able to move quickly,
and may dissuade the attacker from coming too near!

✔ **You go pale and feel cold and clammy.** Blood vessels
near to the skin tighten to reduce any potential blood
loss and sweat glands open to cool down your hard-
working body.

✔ **You don't think, you just react.** The system you usually
use to make decisions and judgements is pushed to the
side and more primitive responses take over.

Of course, when your body reacts in these ways, you may
want to run away from what scares you and avoid going near
it again. The problem with this approach is that you can
become fearful of things that aren't really likely to attack you,
kill you or eat you.

Fear and anxiety develop when your fight, flight and freeze
response becomes connected to something that isn't likely to
cause you the harm that you fear it may.

Every time Bob sees a cat wandering down the street where
he lives, his heart rate and breathing increase, he starts to
sweat and he fears that the cat will attack him. He might see
the cat being stroked by an elderly person or a child, so can
reason with himself that the animal is safe, but he still won't
go near the cat just in case it attacks him.

Furthermore, not only does the original object or situation
result in a fear response, but also other things associated with
the object or situation start to cause the same reaction.

Bob finds that even seeing a cat on the TV or hearing a cat
meow sets off the reaction in his body. He stops going out so
much and, when he does go out, he always keeps a wary eye
out for cats. He turns over TV adverts that feature cats, and
avoids programmes that are more likely to have cat adverts

in the breaks. Although Bob's partner knows of his fear, both she and Bob tend to make a joke of it and have adjusted their lives to reduce the possibility of Bob having any contact with cats.

Bob's fear has started to restrict his life to the extent that he's changed aspects of his daily routine to accommodate his fears. Bob needs to think about tackling his fear rather than adjusting his life and joking about it. If he doesn't, the problem won't go away and Bob's life may become even more restricted.

For more on identifying what scares you, and analysing how you react, take a look at Chapter 2.

Tackling Your Fears in a Manageable Way

In this section we show you how to tackle your fears using a straightforward approach that you can personally adapt to fit your difficulties and the pace at which you'd like to work.

The simple rule is *to do* the things that you've tended to avoid doing and *not do* the things that you'd much rather do, using a one-step-at-a-time, systematic approach – only if it is safe to do so of course!

Constructing a ladder

To face your fears successfully, you start by *gradually* introducing the things you've been avoiding with a view to reducing the amount of anxiety you feel without avoiding or escaping from the feared situations.

Here's a two-step process for starting to tackle your fear (for more on analysing and mapping, head to Chapter 2):

1. **List the things that you've tended to avoid doing because they're associated with your fear.**

2. Put the list(s) in a ladder, from the least hard thing to do to the hardest thing to do.

The top item on your ladder should correspond with your goal for reducing anxiety. Take a look at Chapter 3, which helps you set a SMART goal and understand the anxiety score.

Table 4-1 gives you a Ladder Worksheet you can copy and fill in.

Table 4-1	Ladder Worksheet
Level	*Activity*
10 (hardest – my SMART goal)	
9	
8	
7	
6	
5	
4	
3	
2	
1 (easiest – where I start facing my fear)	

In the previous section we introduced the example of Bob, who is scared of cats. Here's Bob's list of activities he avoids because he associates them with cats.

✔ If possible, I avoid:

- Watching adverts for cat food.
- Touching cats.
- Looking at cats.
- Hearing a cat mew.
- Going out on my own unless in the car.

✔ I try to:

- Carry a small spray bottle of water with me to repel cats if any come too near.
- Be vigilant for cats if I go out, and I ask my wife to keep an eye out too.

Bob's SMART goal (see Chapter 3) was to be able to stroke a cat for a few minutes with an anxiety score of no more than 2.

Table 4-2 shows Bob's Ladder Worksheet.

Table 4-2	Bob's Ladder Worksheet
Level	*Activity*
7 (hardest – my SMART goal)	Touching a cat
6	Going out without carrying a spray bottle of water
5	Going out for a walk on my own without keeping an close eye out for cats
4	Going out for a walk with my wife without asking her to look out for cats
3	Watching adverts for cat food
2	Looking at a cat
1 (easiest – where I start facing my fear)	Listening to a cat mew

When you're tackling fears, you need support, but standing on your own two feet is also important. Sometimes, relying on others for help with your anxiety can keep the anxiety going. In the example, Bob isn't really letting go of his fear if he gives up being so vigilant for cats but his wife carries on keeping an eye out for them on his behalf.

Working your way up the ladder

In the earlier section 'Knowing How Fear Works', we explain how your body reacts to fear. All the physical changes can feel uncomfortable, and that's why doing something scary can be unpleasant. But the thing about the release of chemicals in the fight, flight or freeze response is that the body only has so many of the chemicals and then they start to run out. So if you sit with a fear, you gradually feel less afraid.

You need to systematically work your way up the ladder of your fear. Here's how:

1. **Start at the bottom of the ladder, with the activity that least frightens you.**

2. **Carry out the activity, but don't try to reduce the feeling of anxiety as you do.** If you just stick with the task, then the anxiety comes down of its own accord and your body learns not to respond as if it's threatened.

3. **Keep practising the activity as often as possible.** Ideally, try to practise a couple of times per day.

4. **Chart your progress.** Make a chart or draw your own graph and plot how quickly your anxiety comes down. That way you've a record of your achievements.

5. **When you feel you've conquered your fear, move up the ladder to the next activity.** Take each step in order and don't move on to the next step until you're sure that you've mastered the previous one.

Keep going. Use the anxiety score (see Chapter 3) to check how anxious you feel. Undertaking an activity may push your anxiety score quite high, but it *will* come down. (If your anxiety doesn't come down, make sure that you aren't doing something to try to reduce your anxiety rather than sitting with it. If you do try to reduce your anxiety prematurely, it won't come down naturally.)

Figure 4-1 charts Bob's progress as he takes the first step on his ladder. You can see that:

✔ The first time Bob listens to the cat mew, his anxiety goes up sharply. But he sticks with it and continues to listen, and his anxiety comes down.

✔ The second time, Bob's anxiety level doesn't go as high and it comes down more quickly.

✔ The third time, Bob's even less anxious and his anxiety lessens more quickly still.

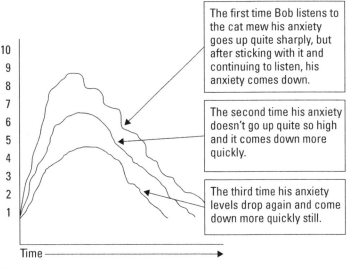

The first time Bob listens to the cat mew his anxiety goes up quite sharply, but after sticking with it and continuing to listen, his anxiety comes down.

The second time his anxiety doesn't go up quite so high and it comes down more quickly.

The third time his anxiety levels drop again and come down more quickly still.

Figure 4-1: Bob's anxiety when listening to a cat mew.

Tackling a fear of blood or needles

For most fears, the fight, flight and freeze reaction makes your blood pressure go up as your arteries constrict and the heart pumps more blood around the body. But if you fear blood or needles, however, you may have a different reaction and go lightheaded and faint.

Some people theorise that fainting at the sight of blood or needles has its roots in helping to save your life, by reducing your blood pressure so you don't lose too much blood if you're injured, or even appearing dead to put off an attacker. But, of course, hitting the deck when your child has a nosebleed or you need a jab is a distressing inconvenience rather than something actually life-saving.

We have two types of treatment for this kind of fear: graded exposure to your fear and applied tension. Both involve facing the thing you're scared of, but they involve extra steps to the approach we outline in the earlier section 'Working your way up the ladder'.

Using the applied tension method

In this method, you raise your blood pressure by doing a series of exercises and then you face the feared situations while working to physically keep your blood pressure raised. If you have any concerns about your blood pressure, or are pregnant, consult your GP before undertaking this method. If this method isn't for you, see 'Going for graded exposure' in the next section.

Here's how to raise your blood pressure:

1. **Standing up, tense your arms, legs and buttocks.** Try to keep your body tensed for 10 to 15 seconds or until you feel your face flushing, and then release the tension.

2. **After about 30 seconds, tense your arms, legs and buttocks again.** Hold for 10 to 15 seconds or until you feel your face flushing, and release.

3. **Repeat five times.** Try to do the exercise five times per day for a week.

When you come to your feared situation, practise this tensing routine. You raise your blood pressure and ward off feeling faint.

Going for graded exposure

This idea is like a conventional ladder. You take a series of steps while facing the feared situation, but in order to help your blood pressure *not* drop, you begin lying down until any anxiety drops and your faintness reduces, and then gradually move your way to being physically upright. You repeat each step until you're able to undertake the task without feeling faint, although you can move on to the next task while you still experience minimal anxiety.

Your ladder might look something like Table 4-3.

Table 4-3	Graded Exposure Ladder Worksheet	
Level	*Activity*	*Steps*
4 (hardest – my SMART goal)	Having an injection or having blood taken	4 Standing
		3 Sitting upright
		2 Sitting up slightly
		1 Lying flat
3	Pricking own finger with a sterilised pin	4 Standing
		3 Sitting upright
		2 Sitting up slightly
		1 Lying flat
2	Looking at a cut on some-one's arm or watching someone else get an injection	4 Standing
		3 Sitting upright
		2 Sitting up slightly
		1 Lying flat
1 (easiest – where I start facing my fear)	Watching a medical pro-gramme on TV	4 Standing
		3 Sitting upright
		2 Sitting up slightly
		1 Lying flat

Work through the ladder in the same way as Bob did in the earlier section 'Working your way up the ladder'.

Whichever strategy you choose to use, remember that practice makes perfect!

Chapter 5

Finding Out if Your Fears Are Fact or Fiction

Sometimes things aren't what they seem. At one time, it seemed that the world was flat. In fact, it does look that way when you're standing on the ground. Ancient scientists looked at the movement of the stars and the planets in the night sky and on the basis of all the facts came up with an alternative theory – that the world is in fact a sphere. However, for many the final proof did not come until ships successfully sailed all the way around the globe.

In this chapter, we're going to ask you to do something similar with your fears – to consider whether they're also not quite what they seem. Such a task may sound as hard for you as it was for people in days gone by to contemplate that the earth wasn't flat. But don't worry; in this chapter we carefully help you through taking a closer look at the facts and gathering more information by testing out your anxieties in real life, like a scientist of fear.

Knowing That Fears Aren't Facts

Just because you think something, doesn't make it a fact.

Imagine that you're all cosy, wrapped up in bed at night, tired and ready to sleep. Your mind is on happy memories and you're just drifting off into a pleasant dream. Suddenly, you hear a loud sound of breaking glass in a downstairs room.

What do you imagine would run through your mind at this point? 'It's someone breaking in', 'An intruder is in my home', or something similar? If so, notice what emotion goes with the meanings that you attach to the sound. Probably, if you think, however fleetingly, that a hostile intruder is causing the noise, you feel pretty scared. Who wouldn't?

Then imagine you go to investigate the sound. It turns out a glass has fallen off the kitchen table and smashed on the floor. Perhaps your cat knocked it off.

What emotion do you feel now, knowing the true explanation? Probably calmer and more settled again? Or maybe a bit cross with your cat!

This exercise shows that the thoughts that you have about events – in other words what the events *mean* to you – affect how you feel about them. When you find out all of the facts, you can sometimes discover that your thoughts aren't completely true and this makes you feel differently. You can discover that you overestimated how likely the worst-case scenario is or how awful it would be, or that you underestimated how well you'd cope with a situation.

Identifying Your Disaster Predictions

What thoughts run through your mind when you're scared? You need to work out the thoughts that keep anxiety going for you, because these thoughts are the ones you explore and test in this chapter. These thoughts may be fleeting or come in the form of a picture in your mind. If you need help identifying scary thoughts, head to Chapter 2 to map your anxiety.

Here are some thoughts that flash into people's minds when they're anxious – we call them *disaster predictions*:

- ✔ If I speak now, I'll go red and people will think I'm an idiot.

- ✔ My heart is going so fast that I'm about to have a heart attack and die.

- ✔ My worries will make me go crazy.

- ✔ If I don't control my anxiety, I'll pass out.

- ✔ I have terminal cancer that has yet to be detected.

- ✔ If I touch anything that hasn't been disinfected, I'll get ill.

- ✔ If I go out of the house, I'll be overwhelmed with anxiety and be unable to get home.

- ✔ If I'm in a confined space, I'll suffocate.

Note down the most important predictions that you make about the worst happening, those that are keeping anxiety going for you. These statements are the ones that flash through your mind at the times of highest anxiety. They're about danger or threat of some sort, and are the sort of statements that, if true, would make anyone nervous. Your disaster predictions may even seem a bit silly to you when you're not anxious, but they're much more believable when you are.

Be specific. Stick to writing down predictions that are specific and testable, like, 'I'll shake, and people will notice and think that I'm pathetic.' Avoid less useful predictions that are:

- ✔ Vague or open to interpretation, like, 'I might make a fool of myself.'

- ✔ Questions, like, 'What will people think of me, if I shake?'

- ✔ Fears about escaping or getting anxious, such as, 'I'll get so anxious that I have to leave'. Going into situations that you may have been avoiding probably will make you feel anxious. The real question is whether some greater catastrophe that you fear will strike if you didn't avoid or escape the situation. So instead, write down the disaster you fear would happen *if you were unable to escape.*

Checking Your Disaster Predictions Against the Facts

You need to take a closer look at your disaster predictions to see whether they fit the all of the facts. Choose one to start with that's particularly bothering you at the moment – one that keeps anxiety going for you.

You can use a six-step process called the Disaster Prediction Fact Checker to check your prediction against the facts (Table 5-1 shows you a filled-in example):

1. **Note the disaster prediction that you want to check.**

   Follow the tips in the earlier section 'Identifying Your Disaster Predictions'.

2. **Determine how anxious you feel about the prediction now.**

   Use a percentage score, with 0 being not at all anxious and 100 as anxious as you've ever felt.

3. **Identify the facts that support the prediction being true.**

   You're looking for factual evidence that supports your idea that this worst-case scenario will come true.

   A good test of whether you're noting down real factual evidence is to ask yourself, 'If I were to stand up in court and try to convince a judge and jury that this prediction is true, would they count this point as factual evidence?'. For example, 'I felt dizzy last time I went to the supermarket' may be a fact, whereas the judge would object if you tried to present this as 'I nearly pass out every time I go out of the house' because you've gone beyond the facts.

4. **Identify the facts that don't completely fit with the prediction being true.**

   Don't be surprised if doing so is tricky because you're looking for facts you've so far overlooked. Ask yourself the following:

- **How likely is the disaster (really) to happen?**
Try to be honest about how likely you think it is
that your disaster prediction will come true. Then
check whether you've overlooked any relevant
facts. Has it ever actually happened to you? Has it
ever happened to anyone? How often has it happened and what really caused it? Is there any hard
evidence, like public records, that tell us anything
about how likely your disaster prediction is?

- **How awful would it be (really)?** Regardless of
how likely the disaster is, how awful you think it
will be has a big impact on how anxious you feel.
See whether you've been overlooking any facts.
Maybe, say, feeling dizzy in a supermarket would
be tough or uncomfortable, but would it definitely
involve the most awful aspects that you imagine?

- **How would I cope (really)?** Some disaster predictions imply that you really wouldn't cope
with the disaster very well. Quite often, people
make anxious predictions about falling apart, not
knowing what to do or completely losing control
of themselves if the feared disaster struck. But
see whether you've overlooked any facts about
how you would actually cope. If it has happened
to you before, how did you actually cope? Can
you learn from this? If it does happen in the
future, what can you do to cope?

Do your research. Sometimes, you won't have
all the information and may need to do extra
research to find facts relevant to your disaster
prediction. For example, if you're afraid of flying
you may need to research how unlikely plane
crashes really are. If you're anxious about blushing,
you may need to find out how few people actually
ridicule those who blush. You can find a lot of
information on the Internet (but use reliable
sources). You can also ask experts or do surveys
of friends or other people who would know.

5. **Make an alternative, balanced prediction.**

You need to come up with an alternative prediction
that takes account of *all* the facts you've noted down
in Steps 3 and 4. Don't be surprised if you find the task
a bit tricky – this way of thinking is new, like grasping

that the world is a sphere, so it may not come to you straight away. Usually, a brief summary of key facts, addressing all the feared aspects of your original disaster prediction, does nicely.

If you struggle to come up with an alternative, think about what a friend would conclude if she saw all these facts laid out. Or maybe even ask a friend to help you.

You don't need to believe this alternative view completely to write it down. In fact, you may well have serious doubts about it. Just make a note of how much you believe the alternative prediction at this point.

6. **How anxious do you feel about the prediction now?**

Again, use a 0–100 scale. Has there been any change? If you believe the alternative, balanced prediction a significant amount, you may find that you now feel a little less anxious about the feared disaster. If not, that's okay too. You're just beginning! But consider whether believing this alternative prediction completely (100 per cent) would reduce your anxiety.

Table 5-1 shows an example of a Disaster Prediction Fact Checker for Donna, who's scared to eat in a restaurant.

Table 5-1   Disaster Prediction Fact Checker

Stage	*Donna's Response*
Disaster prediction	When I eat at the restaurant with my family, I will get so nervous that I'll throw up at the table and people will think I am disgusting.
How anxious do I feel about now? (0–100%)	80%
Facts that support the prediction being true	I get nervous about eating at a restaurant.
	I feel sick when I get nervous.
	I saw someone throw up on a ferry and I found this disgusting.

Stage	Donna's Response
Facts that don't completely fit with the prediction being true	**1. How likely is it really?** I have never actually been sick from nerves. I was sick once at a restaurant but that was probably because I had heatstroke. **2. How awful would it be really?** When I was sick in the restaurant from heatstroke, I did have time to get to the toilets, so no one really knew about it until I came out and told them. **3. How would I cope really?** If I was sick at the table, I would need to just apologise and leave. I would probably not go back to that restaurant, but that wouldn't be the end of the world.
Alternative, balanced prediction	When I eat in a restaurant with my family I may feel sick, but I'm unlikely to actually be sick. Even if I am, I'll probably have time to get to the toilet. Even if the worst did happen, it wouldn't be the end of the world. **How much do you believe this alternative prediction (0–100%)?** 50%
How anxious do I feel about now? (0–100%)	40%

You can use the Disaster Prediction Fact Checker to check any of your disaster predictions. Using it on several predictions is likely be helpful because you can start to build up a big list of useful facts – usually ones that help you feel less anxious. You also get practice at this way of looking for facts, which you can then try when you're *in the situations* that trigger your disaster predictions.

Too much reassurance can be bad for your (mental) health! If your disaster predictions mainly concern your health, beware the temptation to seek reassurance through unnecessary medical investigations or Internet searches for 'facts' about symptoms. If you've had the necessary medical checks and have ruled out a significant physical problem, further searching can be counter-productive, triggering more anxiety rather than providing long-term reassurance. If this situation sounds familiar, take a look at Chapter 6, which gives ideas for how to let go of worry.

Testing Your Disaster Predictions with Experiments

If we said we were going to ask you to do experiments on yourself to test out whether your disaster predictions really would come true, you'd think we were crazy, right? Well, that's exactly what we're going to suggest you do next.

The good news is that experiments can often lead to BIG reductions in anxiety in the long run. The bad news is that you're likely to find the testing a bit scary to start with. Think of the sailor who set out to sail around the world for the first time, not being absolutely sure that it was a sphere. He was probably pretty nervous too, because the disaster prediction was that he would fall off the edge!

Hopefully, you've used the Disaster Prediction Fact Checker that we include in the previous section to work out that the worst-case scenario is less likely or less awful than you thought, or that you may be able to cope better than you were giving yourself credit for. As a result, you may have found that your level of anxiety about the prediction has come down. But having doubts is normal. Maybe, in the cold light of day, you can be confident that the worst won't happen, but when you get into the situation this thinking all goes out the window and you still feel that the worst *is* going to happen?

What you need, as a next step, is to design experiments to test out whether the worst really does happen while you're in the situation that scares you. By finding out the truth, you can break the fear cycle once and for all.

These sorts of experiments are called *behavioural experiments*. They involve *doing* something differently (a behaviour), in order to test out a prediction about what happens.

Key anxiety facts

Some of your disaster predictions may be about catastrophic effects of anxiety itself. When thinking through the facts about disaster predictions, remember the following:

✔ **Anxiety isn't dangerous to your health.** Anxiety causes some uncomfortable physical sensations, but these sensations are normal and none can harm you. (For more on the effect anxiety has on the body, look at Chapter 4.)

✔ **You can't faint because of anxiety.** Although some people feel faint or dizzy when they get anxious, these sensations aren't actually the same as those you get when you faint. Fainting is caused by a drop in blood pressure, but when you're anxious your blood pressure goes up (except with blood phobia – see

Chapter 4). The dizzy sensation you get when anxious is caused by a perfectly safe change in gas balance in the blood when you breathe faster. You can get this dizzy sensation even if you don't notice much change in your breathing, but even breathing really fast won't make you faint.

✔ **Thoughts can't make you go crazy.** You may feel that your thoughts are racing when you feel anxious, or thoughts or pictures are in your mind that you don't like. This feeling can make you afraid that you'll lose control of your mind or act on the thoughts in a crazy way. Anxious thoughts don't make actions happen. Anxiety is more likely to *stop* you doing crazy stuff, because you anticipate the worst possible consequences!

When you picture an experiment, you probably think of professors in white coats, test tubes, rats, bubbling chemicals or explosions. Well, you'll be pleased to know that you don't need any of these things to do an experiment. All experiments are simply ways of testing out how the world really works. You've probably done lots of experiments already today to test a few important questions, like 'Will my car really fit in this small parking space?' or 'Will my hamster eat potato peel?' Experiments are also good for testing out how the world really works compared to how you fear it might work – your disaster predictions.

The builder's apprentice

Have you heard the story about Hamish and the wall? Hamish is an apprentice on a building site. During his first week, the foreman is on holiday and the other builders decide to play a trick on Hamish. 'We have an important job for you,' they say. 'Just stand here and hold this wall up with both hands to stop it falling over – it's weak and may collapse in the heat of the day.' Hamish feels good because he thinks he's been given an important job. At lunchtime, all the other builders go off to a cafe for lunch. They ask Hamish to stay behind and hold up the wall.

On the second day, the same thing happens. By the third day, Hamish doesn't even need to be asked – he just takes up his position and holds up the wall all day. He's pleased with himself because the wall hasn't fallen down.

At the end of the week, the foreman returns from holiday. 'What are

you doing?' he demands. Hamish explains that he's holding the wall to stop it collapsing. 'But this wall is solid; we built it weeks ago!' says the foreman. Hamish isn't convinced. He feels sure that it would have collapsed by now if he hadn't held on to it so well every day.

What could convince Hamish that the wall is solid? Just telling him doesn't seem to be enough. The only real way to convince him would be for him to take his hands off the wall and to see what happens.

In this story, the wall collapsing is a disaster prediction, and holding the wall represents a safety behaviour. Like real safety behaviours, after a while it had become second nature to Hamish. To test Hamish's disaster prediction, he needs to drop his safety behaviour and let go of the wall.

Identifying your safety behaviours

You're being natural and sensible to want do things to try to keep yourself safe, like wearing seatbelts in the car, looking both ways before you cross the road, or checking that food isn't mouldy before you eat it. So, when you're anxious about something you naturally develop ways of doing things that you think can keep you safe from the worst-case disaster. These are *safety behaviours*.

Taking the example of Donna, introduced in the earlier section 'Checking Your Disaster Predictions Against the Facts', some of her safety behaviours are that, on the rare occasions when she eats at a restaurant, she always finds a table near the toilets and only eats a light meal. Safety behaviours make perfect sense if the disaster prediction is true. But they stop you from discovering whether the disaster prediction *really is true* because you never find out what would happen if you didn't carry out the behaviours. To find out the truth about your disaster predictions, you need to experiment with dropping safety behaviours to see what happens. You can take a step-by-step approach by doing a series of experiments in which you gradually drop safety behaviours one by one. You can take it at your own pace and build up your confidence as you go, with each step making the next a little easier.

Table 5-2 gives you examples of disaster predictions, safety behaviours and how you can 'push the wall' (see the nearby sidebar 'The builder's apprentice').

Table 5-2 Steps for Dropping Safety Behaviours

Disaster Prediction	Example Safety Behaviours	Possible Steps for Dropping Safety Behaviours
If my heart goes fast, I'll have a heart attack and die.	Avoid exercise. If I feel anxious, sit down and rest.	1. Do some exercise (if in doubt, check with your doctor first). 2. If I feel anxious, get more active.
Anxiety will make me so sweaty that people will notice and laugh at me.	Wear heavy, dark clothing to hide sweat patches. Avoid eye contact in order not to see people's reactions.	1. Wear comfortable clothing even if it might show sweat. 2. Interact with people, look them in the eye and watch their reactions.

(continued)

Table 5-2 *(continued)*

Disaster Prediction	Example Safety Behaviours	Possible Steps for Dropping Safety Behaviours
If I think about something bad happening, it's more likely to come true.	Keep my mind busy at all times. If 'bad' thoughts come into my mind, think 'good' thoughts to balance them.	1. Let my mind wander. 2. Let 'bad' thoughts come and go without doing anything about them.
Worry will make me ill.	Try to push all worries out of my mind. Drink alcohol to turn the worries off.	1. Let worries come and go without doing anything about them. 2. Reduce my drinking.
I have terminal cancer that all the tests have missed.	Keep returning for repeated tests after I have had all the tests recommended by the doctor and cancer has been ruled out. Spend hours every day looking up symptoms on the Internet.	1. Don't go for repeated tests if my specialist thinks they're unnecessary. 2. Stop looking up symptoms on the Internet.
If I'm in an enclosed area, I'll suffocate.	Open the windows.	1. Close a window. 2. Close all the windows.

Return to your list of disaster predictions and try to identify your safety behaviours – what do you tend to do with the intention of making yourself safe when you're anxious? Make a list of your safety behaviours next to each prediction.

Some people find that they're using prescribed medications as safety behaviours; for example, taking tablets to control anxiety every time you give a talk. Using tablets at the time that anxiety strikes or is feared, with the intention of controlling it can be problematic in the long run because doing so may prevent you from finding out whether your disaster prediction will come true. Taking medication at regular times, such as antidepressants, won't usually interfere with progress using the anxiety-busting methods we give you in this book and can really help some people to get back on track. Don't stop any medication without talking to your doctor first.

Planning and carrying out experiments

Follow these steps when testing your disaster predictions:

1. **Choose the disaster prediction to test.**

   Start with one from your list, or one linked to a particular situation that's coming up. Note how strongly you believe that the prediction will come true.

2. **Work out how you'll know whether the disaster has happened.**

   Be careful that you don't use *how you feel* to judge whether the disaster has happened. For example, *feeling* like you're going to pass out isn't the same as nearly or actually passing out! And if the prediction is about bad stuff happening sometime in the future, be clear about when you'll know if it has happened. For example, if you want to test whether touching a surface and then not washing your hands makes you severely ill, is a day long enough to find out, or two days, or a week?

3. **Decide on a suitable experiment to test whether the disaster prediction is true.**

   This experiment involves putting yourself into a feared situation and dropping safety behaviours. To make it easier, take a gradual approach – drop one safety behaviour for the first experiment, then others as you succeed and gain confidence.

   Some situations really are dangerous, such as driving a motorbike without your usual safety behaviour of keeping your eyes open! So don't design experiments that most people without anxiety difficulties would agree are dangerous. If in doubt, talk to your doctor first. Similarly, if you have a known physical health problem or are significantly overweight and want to test out disaster predictions by changing the amount you exercise, talk to your doctor first.

4. Carry out the experiment.

This part is the scary one. You have two options at this point – carry on living with anxiety that stops you doing things that you want with your life, or take the plunge!

For some experiments, you can enlist a friend or member of your family to help. Just be careful that your companion's presence doesn't get in the way of what you need to find out. For example, you may need to ask the companion not to distract or reassure you. You need to do some experiments alone. If you want to test whether you get so anxious that you scream when you travel on the bus on your own, you obviously can't test this prediction if you're with a friend!

5. Note the outcome of the experiment.

You did it. Well done! Was your disaster prediction correct?

6. Analyse what you've learned.

Having done the experiment, what do you know now that you didn't know before? How much do you now believe the disaster prediction would come true, next time you face a similar situation? Did the outcome support the disaster prediction or an alternative, more balanced conclusion?

Be careful that you don't judge the outcome by how you *feel*. When you're anxious you tend to look out for trouble, which puts a spanner in the works if you're trying to be objective about what's happening in an experiment. Look for facts that would stand up in court. For example, if you're anxious about how people are going to react to you, take care to look at how people are really reacting to you, or ask them, rather than paying attention to how you feel inside. Or if you're worried about how you appear when you do something, ask a friend to take a video of you and then watch it back as if you were watching someone else. Don't use how you feel inside as a sign of how you appear to others!

Good scientists always keep good records! Records help you to think clearly and remember everything important. So we recommend you fill out an Experiment Sheet, like the one we provide in Table 5-3, using Donna as an example.

Table 5-3	Experiment Sheet
Stage	**Donna's Response**
Disaster prediction	When I eat at a restaurant with my family, I will get so nervous that I'm sick and people will think that I'm disgusting.
How you'll know whether the disaster has happened	I'll have vomited and people will have made comments about it being disgusting or will have got up and left.
Experiment	I'll go to eat at a restaurant with my family but also make sure that I don't do the usual safety behaviour of choosing the lightest meal. Sitting near the toilets is another safety behaviour but I'll let myself do this on this occasion.
Outcome	I sat near the toilets and managed to have two courses, but felt full so I didn't have dessert. I did feel a bit sick before the meal, but this feeling went away when an interesting conversation started.
Analysis of learning	I realised that even if I ate until I was full, I didn't vomit. Also, feeling sick doesn't mean I'm going to be sick. I feel more confident that I wouldn't be sick if I ate in restaurants in future. The experiment supports the alternative, balanced view: 'I'm unlikely to be sick from anxiety if I eat at a restaurant, and even if I feel a bit sick I can still enjoy myself.'

Taking the next step

After you've tested one of your disaster predictions once, we're sorry to say that you can't hang up your white coat yet. Most scientists do lots of experiments, not just one! Consider what you still need to test or find out, and design the next experiment. Perhaps you can test the same disaster prediction further, by dropping other safety behaviours or extending the experiment into a new situation. Or perhaps you need to explore other disaster predictions.

Donna decides to try another experiment, going to a restaurant with her family and sitting further away from the toilets. Sitting further away makes her more anxious about the possibility of being sick, but she isn't sick even though she has a full meal. In fact, this time she doesn't even feel sick.

What's your next experiment?

Troubleshooting

The ways that we show you in this chapter of testing out whether your fears are fact or fiction can be powerful tools, but they aren't always easy to master. In case you get stuck, here are some common roadblocks and how you can find ways round them.

I'm too scared to do experiments

Well, we're dealing with anxiety here, so being scared isn't surprising! Can you be gentler with yourself, and start with an experiment that's achievable for you? Maybe you can start without dropping all your safety behaviours at once? Can a friend help you to go forward and take the plunge?

If you're still finding it hard to take that first step, perhaps you can do more work on checking your disaster predictions against the facts. That way you gain more confidence as you feel less sure that the worst is going to happen. But don't be tempted to put off doing things differently until you no longer feel anxious at all. Doing things differently may be the best way to really overcome these fears.

Some of my fears are facts

Recognising that some fears are valid is important. Sometimes anxiety is a good thing. If you're being hunted down by a violent assassin, now isn't the time to do an experiment to test whether you'll be killed when you go out walking the streets! So the bottom line is, we want to work out the reality, not fob you off with an idea that all anxiety is out of proportion.

If you're in real danger, you need to take steps to stay safe. If you're on the receiving end of domestic violence or abuse, for example, you need to get to safety. If you've a serious physical health problem, you need the right investigations and treatment for this.

I'm still not completely convinced

Maybe you've made progress, but still have nagging doubts about whether your disaster predictions are true. Don't worry, this often happens! Remember the story about Hamish and the wall (see the sidebar 'The builder's apprentice'). By taking his hands off the wall Hamish may gain confidence that the wall wouldn't fall down, but an even better test might be to *push* the wall. Doing so would show him once and for all whether it was solid. Are there any further experiments you can do to 'push the wall' by doing the *opposite* of your usual safety behaviours?

For example, after several successful restaurant meals, Donna decided to go to a restaurant with friends who didn't know about her anxiety difficulties, to sit a long way from the toilets and have a full three-course meal. She wasn't sick, and this fact really proved to her that her difficulties were in the past.

Well done! Tackling fears in this way can be scary but can really help to make you feel less anxious in the long run.

Chapter 6

Letting Go of Worry

· ·

In This Chapter

▶ Knowing that worrying is nothing to worry about

▶ Spotting what's fuelling your worry, then cutting off the fuel supply

▶ Transforming worries into problems that you can address

▶ Learning to let go of unsolvable worries

· ·

*W*orry is what happens when you spend time chewing over possible bad stuff that may or may not happen tomorrow, next week or next year. A chain of thoughts or pictures runs through your mind, spreading like a forest fire, with worry about one future 'what if?' scene in your mind setting light to the next, or re-igniting itself again and again. No wonder you can end up physically tense, irritable and exhausted! Worry can be about anything at all, but is often about health, work, money or how you're getting along with people. It often spreads into lots of different topics.

Everyone worries sometimes, usually when something scary or difficult is coming up and they don't know exactly what's going to happen. A little worrying from time to time is natural, but sometimes it can become persistent.

Some of the other methods we have looked at in this book for tackling anxiety may not extinguish persistent worry, so another approach is needed. That's where this chapter helps – we help you take away the fuel for worry, then give you strategies to turn worries into problems you can solve and to let go of the rest.

 Many people who worry a lot also have other anxiety problems like phobias or panic attacks. If this is you, use this chapter alongside Chapters 4 and 5 in this part of the book.

Taking Away the Fuel for Worry

Like a forest fire, worry can't continue if you take away its fuel. In this section, we examine the main fuels for worry and how you can douse them!

Believing that worry is helpful

You do most things because you think they're worthwhile, even if they also have costs. So you may go to the gym because you think it keeps you fit and healthy, even if it costs you money and is painful at the time! Worry is like this too. Even though you may be able to think of lots of costly and painful effects of worry, you may – perhaps secretly – also think that worrying is worthwhile in some way.

Table 6-1 outlines some common views people hold on the pros and cons of worrying.

Table 6-1	The Pros and Cons of Worrying
Pros	*Cons*
Helps me prepare and be ready	Gets me down
Helps me solve problems	Gets me in a muddle
Shows I care	Wastes time
Gets me moving	Stops me sleeping
Helps me cope with bad stuff	Makes me tired, tense and irritable
Keeps me safe	Annoys other people

What are the pros and cons of worry for you? Make your own table, based on your own beliefs about worry. If you could find another way of getting all the things that you hope to gain from worrying, while losing all the bad things that it does for you, would you be keen to try? Of course; who wouldn't! A belief that worry is useful fuels worry.

Try to find other ways of achieving the things you think worry does for you. Put your efforts into finding better ways to show you care, or to prepare for things, or to solve problems. We help you learn a good way of solving problems in the later section 'Following the steps for good problem-solving'.

Trying to avoid uncertainty

Hay fever is caused by an allergy to pollen. Many people have no problem with pollen, whereas others find that when flowers bloom, their eyes start itching and their noses start running.

Persistent worry is like having an allergy to uncertainty. So although many people would be quite happy not knowing exactly what's going to happen, if you've a tendency to worry, you may find this uncertainty really difficult. Uncertain situations open up space for 'what if?'. In fact, lots of research suggests that the harder people find it to put up with uncertainty about things, the more they're likely to be troubled by worry.

The problem is that, like pollen, uncertainty is part of the world that you live in. So you only really have two options – avoid uncertainty as much as possible, or find a way to put up with it.

Unfortunately, trying to avoid uncertainty causes more problems than it solves. For a start, you struggle to make decisions, because doing so involves putting up with some uncertainty – whatever decision you make, you always face a small possibility that your decision may be wrong! If you find this possibility of being wrong hard to live with, the chances are you put off decisions or go round in circles when you think about them.

Removing uncertainty from your life may, in fact, make you miserable. Imagine a life with nothing uncertain in it. You'd never be able to do anything new, meet anyone new or even go out of the house because you can never be certain what any of these things may lead to. So we reckon that finding a way to put up with some uncertainty in your life is the way to go!

See whether you can take this fuel for worry away by deliberately facing uncertainty – go towards things with uncertain outcomes rather than away from them. For example, try a new sport, go a different way to work, or try a few new recipes. You can't be sure how these things will work out, but by avoiding them, you can be sure that you can't live life to the full. Can you see uncertainty as exciting, the spice of life, even if it's a little scary too?

Trying to control thoughts

If you worry a lot, you probably get pretty sick of thinking about all the bad things that might happen. Some of the possibilities are pretty frightening – someone you know may be run over by a bus, or you may lose all your money, or you may fail at the project you're working on. So the natural reaction is to try to push these worrisome thoughts out of your mind.

The polar bear experiment can tell you whether trying to push thoughts or pictures out of your mind really helps or not. Here's what you do:

1. **Sit down somewhere quiet, close your eyes and spend two minutes trying as hard as you can *not* to think about polar bears.**

   If pictures of polar bears come into your mind, do whatever you can to force them out. Imagine that your life depends on it.

2. **Close your eyes again, but this time spend two minutes thinking about whatever you want.**

   If polar bears happen to come into your mind that's okay, and if they don't that's fine too.

3. **When you've finished, notice how much you thought about polar bears in each phase, and what the thoughts or images were like in each phase.**

Only read on when you've done the experiment! Now, bear with us . . .

Most people say that they have more thoughts of polar bears when they try to *stop* the thoughts, or that there was really little difference. Interestingly, many people also find that the pictures or thoughts of polar bears are more disturbing or distressing when they're trying to force them away. When we tried this experiment with one of our clients, he told us that when he tried *not* to think of polar bears he pictured polar bears attacking him, but when he allowed the thoughts his mind wandered onto feeding baby polar bears with a bottle! Occasionally, someone does manage to force the thoughts of polar bears out of his mind completely – but doing so takes a lot of effort and attention. Doing it all the time would get in the way of normal life.

The polar bear experiment shows you that trying to control or suppress thoughts of bad stuff is a bit like picking up the nearest bucket and chucking its contents on the worry fire, but then finding out the bucket was full of petrol!

 Try to give up thought control because thought control is another fuel for worry. Can you let thoughts pass through your mind without latching on to them, even if they're frightening? We give you more tips on how to achieve this in the later section 'Letting Go of Unsolvable Worries'.

Turning Some Worries into Problems You Can Solve and Letting Go of the Rest

You've cut off the fuel supply for worry. Now when you notice a worry, follow these steps, which we cover in detail in this section:

- ✔ Work out what you're worried about.

- ✔ Try turning *'what if?'* and *'why?'* worries into *'how?'* and *'what?'* questions that you can do something about. Then follow the steps for good problem-solving.

- ✔ For worries that you can't do anything about, learn to let go of the worry and pay attention to something more useful.

Turning 'what if?' and 'why?' into 'how?' and 'what?'

Most worries are about 'what if?' questions. In other words, they're about possibilities – things that may or may not happen in the future. Like 'What if I run out of petrol on the way to the supermarket?' and 'What if my child is ill while she's at a sleepover?'

Perhaps you also chew over 'why?' questions, particularly when you feel down. These questions tend to be about yourself or how the world works, like, 'Why am I always feeling down like this when really I shouldn't be?'

Darryl is on his way to an important job interview when his car breaks down. He sits in his broken-down car saying to himself, 'What if the interview panel think I don't want the job, or that I've rudely not bothered to turn up on time?' Then he starts to think, 'Why does this sort of thing always happen to me?'

How helpful do you think these sorts of questions are for Darryl in solving the problem he has – that he's late for his interview? Of course, they're not helpful. Even if Darryl finds answers to the questions, they won't solve the problem! What can Darryl ask himself instead that can help him to solve his problem? 'How can I get a message to the panel?' or 'What can I do to get there?' may help.

Keep a diary of your worries for a week. Don't write too much, just a sentence for each worry. Then ask yourself:

✔ How many of the worries are of the 'what if?' or 'why?' type?

✔ How many are about 'how?' or 'what?' questions?

✔ Looking at your completed worry diary, how many 'what if?' and 'why?' worries can you turn into 'how?' and 'what?'

The worries that you can turn into 'how?' and 'what?' magically become problems that can be solved. For example, 'What if I run out of conversation when I am speaking?' can turn into 'What are the top three interesting topics I can talk about?' or 'How can I be confident enough to just go with the flow of the conversation?' Practise the skill of turning 'what if?' and 'why?' into problems that you can solve.

Following the steps for good problem-solving

When you've identified a problem, how do you solve it? Chances are, if you've always had a tendency to worry, you may be worried about this! If you've an allergy to uncertainty, solving problems can be tricky because you may put off tackling them or making decisions. Avoiding tackling problems means that you don't tend to sort them out very well, and this result gives you the idea that you're not good at problem-solving, which can put you off even more.

We take you through the steps of effective problem-solving. We suggest you start with a fairly simple problem that doesn't worry you too much; then work up to the bigger, scarier ones as you get used to the process.

Here are the steps of effective problem-solving:

1. **Identify the problem to be solved.**

   Write a brief description of the problem. A sentence or two is normally enough. A solvable problem often starts with 'How' or 'What'. Avoid starting with 'What if' or 'Why' (see the section 'Turning 'what if?' and 'why?' into 'how?' and 'what?'' to be sure that you're not trying to solve an unsolvable problem).

2. **List all possible solutions.**

   Write down briefly all the possible solutions you can think of, even if some or all have disadvantages. Think broadly here, but don't get stuck chewing solutions over too much – just get as many possible ideas down on paper as you can. For each solution on the list, note down the pros and cons.

3. **Choose the best solution to try.**

   You can probably spot and rule out some of the ideas that you can see are going to make things worse. But many possible solutions have pros and cons, or things that are as yet uncertain about them. Given the information you have *now*, pick the best path forward to try, or at least to investigate further. It doesn't matter if the solution you choose won't completely solve the problem – maybe it can be a step in the right direction.

   Choosing the right solution to try is tricky. You'll need to live with some uncertainty here. After all, you can't know 100 per cent for sure whether the solution is a good one until you try it! But the good thing is, being wrong is okay: you get a second chance if the first solution doesn't work.

The nagging parrot

Have you heard the story of Wendy and Wotif? Wotif is Wendy's pet parrot. He is attached to Wendy and always sits on her shoulder wherever she goes. Wotif can speak but everything he says starts with 'what if'. Wherever Wendy goes, you can hear Wotif talking in her ear: 'What if they don't like you at the party and no one talks to you?', 'What if you don't get all your work done on time?', 'What if you never find a boyfriend?' and so on.

Of course, this sort of talk makes Wendy pretty anxious. So she starts to argue back – 'Some people do like me, and that time when no one talked to me was probably because they all knew each other already' and so on. But what effect do you think this has on Wotif? He loves all the attention and just comes up with more and more 'what ifs' – 'But what if you've become boring now that you're older and what if everyone at *this* party knows each other already?'

And so the argument goes on. Wendy can't get rid of the parrot. She tries telling him to shut up, but this rebuke just makes him angry and more troublesome. In the end, Wendy decides to try a new way – she lets Wotif speak, but she just quietly acknowledges the uncertainty that Wotif is telling her about and then gets on with what she needs to do. So when Wendy is at work and Wotif says 'What if your boss thinks you're not trying hard enough', she just listens and quietly answers, 'Yes, maybe – we can't be sure about that can we?' Then she gets on with her work. In this way, Wotif usually runs out of things to say pretty quickly and is much less trouble.

4. **Make a plan and do it.**

   Yes, you can't put it off any longer! You need to put your money where your mouth is. If not now, plan for when.

5. **Evaluate what happened.**

   Did you solve the problem, or at least move things forward? What did you learn? Did you find out anything about other possible solutions?

6. **If you didn't solve the problem or move things forward, follow the process again.**

   By the way, step 6 doesn't mean you failed! It means the problem-solving method is working – it helps you try things one by one rather than getting stuck before you start. Maybe you're now clearer about the real nature of the problem that you need to solve, or are ready to try a different solution to the problem.

Follow the format in Table 5-1 and write down your problem-solving until it becomes second nature. Writing it down in this format helps to stop you getting sidetracked onto other what if? questions as you're going along.

Table 6-2 shows an example of the steps of problem-solving for Brian, who's worried about who's going to look after his dog while he's in hospital.

Table 6-2	Problem-solving Steps
Stage	*Brian's Response*
Problem to be solved	How can my dog Jack be taken care of when I go into hospital for a few days for an operation?
All possible solutions	1. Ask my friend to look after Jack for a few days.
	PROS – Option is free, my friend lives nearby.
	CONS – My friend is out at work all day and Jack will be alone.
	2. Book Jack into kennels.
	PROS – I won't have to ask a favour of anyone.
	CONS – It costs money, Jack doesn't like it there.
	3. Ask my daughter to have Jack.
	PROS – Jack would be happy, my daughter is coming down to drop me at the hospital, so can take Jack back with her.
	CONS – My daughter lives two hours' drive away so getting Jack back may be tricky.

(continued)

Table 6-2 *(continued)*

Stage	Brian's Response
The best solution to try	Ask my daughter whether she can have Jack.
The plan for doing it	I'll ring my daughter now and ask her and see whether she would mind also bringing Jack back when I come out of hospital.
What happened	My daughter said she wouldn't mind having Jack but won't be able to bring him back until a week after the operation. This is fine with me as it gives me a chance to recuperate at home before I need to take Jack for walks again.

Mastering a skill like problem-solving takes practice. Be careful that you don't get distracted by 'what if?' thinking, or by ideas that problem-solving won't work for you. Remind yourself that absolute certainty is impossible and that only by practising can you solve problems effectively. Sadly, not all problems have a really good solution, just the best solution out of several that you don't like much. But the best of several bad solutions is still better than no solution at all! Sometimes, all you can do is partially solve a problem or take a first step in the right direction.

Letting Go of Unsolvable Worries

You can't turn all worries into problems that you can solve. Some 'what ifs' remain, even when you've done everything you can to turn them into solvable problems. For example, perhaps you're still bothered by 'What if I never meet anyone I want to spend my life with?' even if you're doing what you can to find a partner. Or you may be bothered by 'What if I fail my exams?' even if you're revising hard. Letting go of this nagging and bullying from unsolvable worries is a big firebreak you can put up to stop the fire of worry.

Letting go is different to trying to force the unsolvable worries out of your mind and never think about them. Letting go is about noticing the worries, acknowledging the uncertainty or even letting yourself think about the worst that could happen, but not letting the worries rule your life.

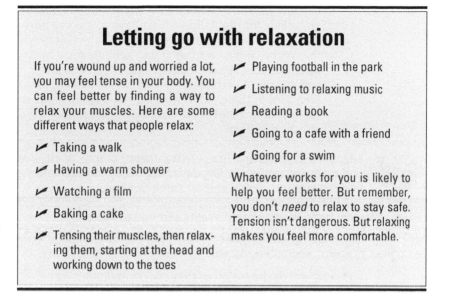

Letting go with relaxation

If you're wound up and worried a lot, you may feel tense in your body. You can feel better by finding a way to relax your muscles. Here are some different ways that people relax:

✔ Taking a walk

✔ Having a warm shower

✔ Watching a film

✔ Baking a cake

✔ Tensing their muscles, then relaxing them, starting at the head and working down to the toes

✔ Playing football in the park

✔ Listening to relaxing music

✔ Reading a book

✔ Going to a cafe with a friend

✔ Going for a swim

Whatever works for you is likely to help you feel better. But remember, you don't *need* to relax to stay safe. Tension isn't dangerous. But relaxing makes you feel more comfortable.

Here are the three steps that allow you to let go of unsolvable worries:

1. Live with uncertainty.

Acknowledge the uncertainty of the situation. When you think of the 'what if?', rather than arguing with it, agree with it – say to yourself, 'Well, it's true that I can't be certain about that'. Remember, uncertainty is a part of life – rather than getting away from uncertainty, put your energy into coping with it.

2. Let worries come.

Notice worries, but without engaging or arguing with them. Don't be tempted back into some kind of thought control with unsolvable worries. Thought control is like arguing with Wotif or trying to push him off your shoulder (see the nearby sidebar 'The nagging parrot'). Thought control makes things worse. Instead, let the worst-case scenario come into your mind. A worry can't hurt you!

3. Let worries go.

Do you want to spend your life paying attention to a stupid bullying parrot (see the nearby sidebar 'The nagging parrot'), or to other really good stuff, like your grandkids, or the daffodils that have just come into flower? We know what we'd choose. You've noticed the worry; move on to what you actually need to pay attention to – like the conversation you're in, the report you're writing or the sausage you're cooking. Like a lot of things in this book, letting go of worries takes practice and perseverance. Hang in there – it's worth the effort!

Imagine this scenario. You're in a railway station. Trains are pulling in and out every few moments. When a train comes into the station, you've at least three options:

- ✔ Stand in front of the trains and try to stop them.
- ✔ Stop the trains from leaving until you've examined every nut and bolt in detail.
- ✔ Just watch the trains as they pull in and out.

Which one of these three options lets the rail network run smoothly? Now suppose the station is your mind and the trains are worries. What do you currently do when the trains pull into the station? Can you try just to watch them pull in and out?

Chapter 7

Anxiety Rules and How to Break Them

In This Chapter

▶ Identifying recurring patterns of thinking that maintain anxiety

▶ Knowing that being human means not being perfect

▶ Letting go of unhelpful rules and relinquishing the need to control

*E*veryone employs certain rules to live by. Some rules are helpful and save you time and energy in new situations; others are unhelpful and cause you to make assumptions about yourself, the world and the future. Such unhelpful rules stop you doing the things that you really value and contribute to your anxiety.

This chapter describes how unrealistic or unhelpful rules for living play a role in anxiety, and how you can overcome them. We help you to identify patterns in your thoughts and actions that might be driven by anxiety rules. Then we explain how you can break unrealistic and unhelpful rules and try out more flexible and compassionate ways of thinking about yourself and other people.

 Don't be surprised if some of what you read in this chapter sounds wrong – or even makes you feel a little anxious. If unhelpful and unrealistic rules are underpinning your patterns of behaviour, you may have been ruled by them for a long time and believing differently takes time.

Identifying Anxiety Rules

In order to make sense of the world and act effectively within it, we develop rules to live by. Your rules are learned from experience. For example, when you get to a red light you know to stop because you learned this rule. The rules you hold underpin your expectations about the world around you. You assume that the red light rule is also shared by other people, so you feel safe to walk onto a crossing when the traffic has a red light. The rule is useful because it saves valuable time and energy – you don't need to wonder what to do at a red light, you can automatically apply the rule 'Stop at a red light' when you're driving and act on this instinctively.

You have different kinds of rules:

- ✔ **Shared with your culture:** Don't drink and drive, and clean your teeth before you go to bed, for example.

- ✔ **Shared with your family:** Eat your greens, or write a thank-you card if you receive a gift are examples.

- ✔ **Unique to you:** For example, exercise three times a week or double-check travel reservations. You develop these rules from your own unique learning history.

You may not be consciously aware of what your rules are, or how they influence you. You may subconsciously treat rules as basic facts of life and act on them accordingly. But rules aren't facts; they're just guides you've learned to save the time and energy of making new decisions in familiar situations.

Much of the time these rules provide helpful shortcuts to making decisions and navigating the world. However, some rules, when applied too rigidly, can be problematic and maintain anxiety. These are *anxiety rules*.

Anxiety rules are ideas that you hold about yourself, other people or the world that generate or maintain anxiety. They're usually inflexible, strict and unrealistic. They aren't helpful, because you can't stick by them, and this inability makes you feel bad. For example, the idea: 'I shouldn't make mistakes', if applied rigidly, may be an anxiety rule because it's only human to make mistakes from time to time.

Anxiety rules often take an extreme position:

- ✔ 'I must always . . . '
- ✔ 'I should never . . . '

or dictate what you can or can't do in a given situation:

- ✔ 'If I do this, then . . . '
- ✔ 'If I don't do that, then . . . '

and they tend to follow common themes. Table 7-1 lists some common examples of anxiety rules.

Table 7-1   Common Themes of Anxiety Rules

Theme of Anxiety Rule	Example
High standards	'I must always be the best at everything I do.'
	'I should never make mistakes.'
Acceptability	'If I stutter or blush when talking to people, they will think badly of me.'
	'I must always be funny or no one will like me.'
Vulnerability/ Weakness	'I can't go to new places or try new things on my own.'
	'If something goes wrong, I won't be able to cope.'
Control	'I must always be in control of my emotions.'
	'If I don't plan for every possible problem, I will fail.'

Anxiety rules are unrealistic and can make unreasonable demands of you or others ('I must never let anyone down', 'I should get the highest grade in all my classes', 'Other people ought to be courteous at all times', 'Life should be fair'). You know that you've found an anxiety rule when you feel very uncomfortable when you imagine not following the rule. If you imagine that a disaster would occur if you didn't follow the rule, you can use the Disaster Prediction Fact Checker in Chapter 5 to check this prediction out.

Having guiding principles to live by isn't a problem – in fact they can be helpful – but when these principles become rules that are inflexible, unrealistic or unreasonable, they can really add to your anxiety.

Finding Patterns

In Chapter 2 we guide you to make a map of anxiety, noticing your thoughts, feelings, bodily reactions and behaviour when you feel most anxious or distressed. We also suggest that you record your reactions to upsetting situations over a whole week. Now, you can use the information you've gathered to identify some of the rules and assumptions that may be maintaining your anxiety.

You can use your map and anxiety diary to uncover patterns in your thinking and behaviour in two ways:

- ✔ Look at your anxiety diary over the course of a week to see whether you can identify patterns of thinking or responding that keep cropping up.

- ✔ Choose one diary entry from the week that you found particularly difficult in some way and think about other times when you've felt this way, what you were thinking about and how you responded.

When you're exploring your anxiety diary, look for repetitions or patterns in your thinking because these repetitions can indicate more deep-rooted rules and assumptions about yourself and the world around you that may be maintaining your anxiety.

Do you notice any patterns in your thinking associated with feeling anxious? Write down your ideas. Don't think about right or wrong answers, just give it a go.

Joanne is good at her job and well-liked by colleagues, but often feels anxious when speaking in meetings or giving presentations at work. Looking at her anxiety diary, Joanne noticed that the thought that crosses her mind at these times usually involves messing up and being thought badly of by her boss and her colleagues. She feels very anxious when she makes a mistake at work. This pattern suggests that Joanne may have a rule about keeping high standards: 'I must always be excellent at work.'

Simon enjoys spending time with his new girlfriend, but worries a lot that it won't last. Simon calls and texts his girlfriend all the time, and tries hard to do the right thing and make her like him. He feels particularly anxious when she doesn't answer her phone and wonders if she has gone off him. He recalls similar anxieties in other new relationships. This pattern suggests that Simon may have a rule about acceptance: 'I have to work hard to be liked, or I'll be rejected.'

Karen feels anxious when visiting new places, especially if she has to take public transport to get there. She spends a lot of time checking timetables, and always leaves home well in advance. She finds it difficult to accept that she may arrive somewhere late, and spends a lot of time analysing all of things she should have done differently to prevent the delay. This pattern suggests that Karen may have some rules about being in control – for example 'If I'm fully in control, then I can prevent bad things from happening.'

In order to see whether you stick to unhelpful rules and assumptions, ask yourself some questions:

- ✔ Do you tend to set high standards for yourself and believe that you should try to do the best you can in almost everything you do?

- ✔ Do you worry a lot about other people's opinion of you, and expect to be scrutinised and found wanting by your family, colleagues, friends or partner?

- ✔ Do you regularly feel anxious if you're not in control of events around you, and believe that if you're in control you can ensure that bad things won't happen?

Answering yes to any one or all these questions suggests that you have anxiety rules that may be maintaining patterns of responding to experiences and keeping you feeling anxious.

 If you've been anxious for a while, you may struggle to define your anxiety rules because, having lived by them for so long, they've become mental habits and part of who you are. It may be helpful to recruit a friend or family member to help you see the patterns that you don't notice for yourself and offer a different point of view.

Asking for help is a sign of strength, not a sign of weakness. People generally like helping others.

The following sections outline some common themes in anxiety rules: perfection, acceptance and control.

Being perfect

Perfectionists strive to do their very best at everything, whatever the circumstances and whatever the cost – and this striving has a robust association with anxiety. Unlike healthy enthusiasts, perfectionists tend to over-invest in achievement-focused activities, and ultimately take little pleasure in the things that they do.

Anxiety rules along the lines of 'I must do everything perfectly' are common. We hate to break it to you, but nobody is perfect. You're not perfect, and neither are the people you love, the people you work with, or even your heroes – no one can be perfect in every way. Being human means being flawed: you can't be the best at everything, and from time to time everyone makes mistakes. Realising that you're not perfect, and that no one else expects you to be, might be quite a relief!

Being accepted

People who have rules about being accepted by others often believe that they're not good enough to be liked or loved without working hard to be accepted and approved of by other people. They perceive their social world to be fragile and worry that if they mess up in any way, they'll be judged harshly and rejected. Rules about acceptability often take conditional forms: 'If people see the real me, I'll be rejected' or 'If I do all the right things, people will like me.' These kinds of rules mean that people tend to over-monitor their social behaviour, which may leave them feeling and even looking awkward. Trying too hard to be accepted can hinder rather than help developing relationships.

Acceptability rules are associated with high self-criticism and low self-compassion. Learning to accept yourself, without conditions, is a healthy step towards overcoming anxiety. We hope this book is helping you to be compassionate with yourself.

Being in control

A particularly common anxiety rule is that 'I need to be fully in control'. People who have this rule often also believe that if they're not fully in control of events then catastrophic things will happen. Control rules often lead to investing excessive effort in planning future activities and controlling everything (and everyone!) around you.

Actually, you can't control everything, and this fact is where a strict control rule becomes unrealistic and unhelpful. Other people, task demands and environmental factors (for example, time of day and weather) all contribute to the way the world works. Unexpected things happen in life, and although accepting the unexpected in the shorter term may feel quite anxiety provoking, in the longer term life is easier and you feel less anxious.

To find your rules for living, you need to explore the patterns that keep coming up in your thinking and responses. Are you regularly trying to control things and plan for every eventuality? If so, then breaking your control rules may help to reduce your anxiety in the longer term.

Breaking the Rules

The following sections give you plenty of strategies for combating unhelpful rules by developing more realistic guides to life, to accepting good enough when it's good enough, from dropping self-criticism to accepting yourself compassionately.

Developing more helpful rules

Being more realistic about what you can expect of yourself, other people and the world around you is one key to overcoming the pressures of anxiety rules. If you've a rigid rule that contributes to your anxiety, building a more balanced version of the rule can help to overcome this.

1. **Identify a rule that you'd like to work on.**

   Write it down in the form of a rule, for example, 'I should be fully up-to-date with every project'.

2. List the advantages and disadvantages of this rule for you.

How does this rule serve you? What problems does this rule cause for you? What would life be like if you broke this rule? Would following a more flexible, realistic guide improve your situation?

3. Create a more realistic rule.

What would be a more realistic, helpful and adaptive rule? Consider using more flexible and less extreme terms (try 'sometimes' instead of 'always', 'prefer' instead of 'should', 'some people' instead of 'everyone').

Your more helpful rule could be: 'I prefer to keep up-to-date on most projects.'

4. Put this new rule into practice.

Give it a try, and notice what effect it has. Adjust your new rule if you need to so that it works best for you. Realistic rules tend to be longer and more sophisticated than anxiety rules and may include a few exceptions – are there some situations where you won't follow your rule (say, if you're on leave)?

To revisit the examples from the previous section 'Finding Patterns', Joanne, Simon and Karen's rules change into something like this:

- ✔ 'I must always be excellent at work' changes to 'I try to do my best most of the time when I'm at work. If a project isn't so important, I'll devote less time to it, so I can prioritise my most important projects and not burn-out.'

- ✔ 'I have to work hard to be liked, or I'll be rejected' changes to 'I'll be myself and hope that people I like also like me most of the time.'

- ✔ 'If I'm fully in control, then I can prevent bad things from happening' changes to 'I accept that some things are out of my control.'

Being good enough

Perfectionists live by the rule that they must do everything to a high standard, but the rule means that they often take longer to complete a task than most people, and achieve less. For example, perfectionists may stay late at work and work on projects for much longer than other colleagues. The long-term costs outweighs the short-term benefits: focusing all of your efforts on doing just a few tasks really well may mean that you're missing out on lots of other things you could be doing, and working longer hours can lead to exhaustion in the longer term.

Rather than being perfect, being good enough may be good enough. What we mean is that being the very best isn't always the best strategy – so thinking flexibly about what's required for different tasks can help you to combat your anxiety rules. Flexible thinking means applying different standards to different tasks – some activities benefit from your best efforts, others may require less scrutiny.

Allowing yourself to do something that's below your normal standard can help you to check out how realistic your high expectations are. Being good enough means being realistic about limitations – and in the longer term you achieve more with less anxiety.

So you leave the superhero stuff – super strength, speed, endurance and rigid moral codes – to comic books and legends. When you find yourself trying to be a superhero (saying yes to more tasks than is feasible at work, never making mistakes, being in control of everything and responsible for everyone else whatever they're doing), you need to find a way to resist.

Make a list of some of the tasks you need to complete during the coming week (for example, prepare a presentation at work, choose a gift for a friend's birthday, sort out the cupboard under the stairs and so on). Now, make a note next to each of these tasks what would be a reasonable amount of time to spend completing that activity (for example, 3 hours, 20 minutes, 90 minutes, respectively). Now, just as an experiment, try to stick to those timings when you work on these tasks next week. Make a note of how easy, or difficult you find it to stick to the timings. What can you learn from this activity about the standards you set yourself and being good enough?

Getting the balance right with criticism

Because anxiety rules are rigidly held, when you break a rule you may often be highly self-critical. Striving for high standards may mean that 'nothing less will do', that tiny mistakes – whether you notice them, or someone else does – are amplified, and that you lambast any error or deviance from the 'right way of doing things'.

Consider whether you find yourself being self-critical following a mistake or failure. Is your self-criticism constructive, realistic and helpful – or does it just make you feel bad? Do you notice any differences between how you respond to yourself and how you respond to a friend if she makes the same mistake? Are you more forgiving or more understanding to the friend? Can you turn this kindness on yourself next time you make an error?

Being more compassionate towards yourself when you get things wrong is an important step in overcoming perfectionism.

Noticing what you've achieved

If you're prone to perfectionism, you may spend so much time focusing on getting things right that you forget to notice what you've achieved and to recognise that things are going well. Try to make time to notice what you've achieved, and don't dismiss small things. Feeling satisfied with the achievement of realistic goals is a big step towards overcoming perfectionism.

Noticing what you've achieved is harder than remembering the things you haven't. Keep a notebook, and make a note each day of something that went well for you. Review your successes at the end of each week – and reward yourself for these.

Making mistakes with confidence

Everyone makes mistakes, so accepting this fact in respect of yourself and other people makes life easier. Far from being a sign of failing or weakness, making mistakes makes you human and helps you to grow and develop.

Great mistakes

Penicillin is one of the most important, life-saving drugs in the world – and it was discovered by accident when Alexander Fleming noticed a mould growing on dishes that had been left accidentally unsterilised in his laboratory. He noticed that no germs were growing near the mould, and went on to discover that this mould – penicillin – could fight deadly bacteria without harming human tissue and so had a wide application to fighting infection and disease.

Many homes and offices have a ready supply of Post-it notes – they're one of the most common office supplies and generate a healthy revenue for the 3M company. But Post-it notes were originally invented by mistake by an engineer hoping to create a super-sticky glue for use in space craft. He was disappointed by the poor adhesion of his new product. It wasn't until several years later that a colleague recognised the potential for low-adhesion sticky notes and began a marketing campaign that made them a household name.

So remember – so-called mistakes can actually be wonderful learning opportunities!

Anxious people tend to overestimate the consequences of their own blunders. In reality, few disasters occur following small mistakes, and other people are more forgiving than anxious people expect. And if you're not convinced, research has found that people who make mistakes are rated as more likable and more approachable than those who get everything right.

People holding high standards sometimes find it hard to try new things, because they feel anxious that they'll make a mistake or not be good at it. So instead of seizing opportunities, perfectionists avoid or put off trying new things, which reduces anxiety in the short term but also reduces the chances of having enriching and enjoyable experiences.

Some of the most important learning opportunities you have come from making mistakes. Just because something doesn't work, doesn't mean that you can't learn from it. In fact, some of the most important progress is made on learning from things that seem to have gone wrong – that's how we got Post-it notes and penicillin (see the nearby sidebar on this).

If you feel anxious about what other people think of you or of what you think of yourself if you don't meet high standards, try making a mistake on purpose.

1. **Imagine yourself in a situation where you'd normally strive for perfection.**

   For example, you may choose giving a presentation at work or attending a social gathering.

2. **Think of a mistake that you might make in that situation.**

   Try to think of something that makes you feel at least mildly anxious, such as having spelling mistakes in your presentation, forgetting someone's name or wearing your top inside out.

3. **Imagine the outcome.**

   What would happen? How would others react? What would you think, and how would you feel?

4. **Deliberately make the mistake and notice what really happens.**

   Did your fears about other people's reactions come true? Did anything unexpected happen? What can you take from the experience about making mistakes? Head to Chapter 5 for more info on testing out your predictions.

Accepting yourself

Being emotionally healthy means accepting yourself for who you are. Find the things that you like about yourself and you admire in other people and try to enjoy these things and be content with who you are.

Make a list of three things that you value about yourself; for example, I am kind, I can cook, I love my son. Try to find a daily example of how one of these qualities has served you well on that day.

Being kind to yourself

Making changes can be hard. Being kind to yourself while you're trying to change and keeping this kindness up throughout your life helps you to weather many storms. Developing belief in yourself as a unique, valued individual can help you to galvanise your strength to move forward in tackling your anxiety. Give your self-esteem and self-confidence a boost by considering these ideas:

✓ **Self-talk:** Talk to yourself as you would to others – what would you say to someone else who was struggling with anxiety?

✓ **Self-compassion:** Offer yourself support, care and kindness.

✓ **Self-confidence:** Believe that you hold the strength in you to move towards your goal to overcome anxiety and live the life you want without being constrained.

Letting go of the reins

For some people, feeling in control of their activities and the events around them is extremely important. Imagine something that you like to control, like packing the suitcases for your summer holidays. How would you feel about letting someone else do that for you? What do you imagine would happen if you weren't in control of that task? If you feel uncomfortable, control may be a problem for you.

Combating anxiety rules to do with control involves letting go of the reins. This letting go may mean someone else picks the reins up or that no one takes them, and discovering that unexpected, but not disastrous, things happen.

Letting go of the reins is rarely terrible. Other people can be more competent than you think – or they might learn to be, given the chance to practise!

You can influence the way that you feel and act even when you can't control the events around you.

Pass over a task to someone else; for example, organising a meeting or planning a weekend activity. Make a note of what you expect to happen, and then compare your prediction to what actually does happen. Even if the outcome isn't what you expected, is it really so bad?

Old habits die hard

Letting go of the rules you've lived by for a long time can be hard. Give yourself the chance to develop a new approach by considering these ideas:

✔ **Be patient.** Learning a new way of being takes time.

✔ **Notice progress.** Every little helps.

✔ **Don't give up.** A little practice every day helps you to overcome unhelpful rules for living and build confidence in being just as you are.

Part III
Making Progress and Moving On

ATTEMPTING TO REDUCE THE ANXIETY IN HIS LIFE, WALDO "WHIP" GUNSCHOTT GOES FROM BEING A WILD ANIMAL TRAINER, TO A WILD BALLOON ANIMAL TRAINER..

In this part . . .

There's more to you, and more to life, than anxiety. In this part, you put anxiety into context. You look at common obstacles to positive change and how to build a happier, healthier life. Finally, you consider how far you've already come in overcoming anxiety with CBT, and set your satnav for a brighter future ahead.

Chapter 8

Looking at the Bigger Picture

*T*here's more to you than your anxiety. You're a complex and multifaceted human being and your experience of anxiety is only one small part of the bigger picture. For some people, anxiety is a single blot on the landscape that stands alone and can be tackled independently. For others, anxiety is intertwined with other problematic thoughts, feelings and behaviours that make moving forward more difficult or even contribute to the anxiety itself.

This chapter puts anxiety into perspective. We discuss some of the common problems that may co-occur with or contribute to your anxiety: low mood or depression, troubled sleep, unrealistic concerns about responsibility, and problems with alcohol or prescription medication. Then we explain how keeping a healthy lifestyle, doing more of the things that you enjoy and nurturing healthy relationships can help you to feel good and keep on top of anxiety. Letting go of unhelpful habits and taking care of yourself physically, mentally and socially builds your resilience for tackling anxiety and helps you to make the most out of life when the burden of anxiety is out of the way.

Going further afield: More helpful resources

If, after reading this book, you feel that you would benefit from extra help, try these useful resources:

Books:

✔ *Mind Over Mood: Change How You Feel By Changing the Way You Think* by Christine Padesky and Dennis Greenberger (1995, Guildford Press).

✔ *The Worry Cure: Stop Worrying and Start Living* by Robert Leahy (2005, Piatkus).

✔ *Overcoming Anxiety* by Helen Kennerley (1997, Robinson).

Websites:

✔ www.llttf.com A free self-help website about living life to the full.

✔ www.anxietyuk.org.uk The Anxiety UK website, which lists their free helpline.

✔ www.nopanic.org.uk The No Panic website includes a helpline and other resources available free or for a minimal fee.

✔ www.fearfighter.com An evidence-based programme for overcoming panic and phobias.

Services and therapists

✔ NHS Choices (www.nhs.uk) helps you find local services to help with anxiety and provides video stories from people who have had a talking therapy such as CBT.

✔ To find a private CBT therapist (who you would pay to see) search www.cbtregisteruk.com.

Handling Problems That Can Accompany Anxiety

Anxiety is a stand-alone problem for many people, but for others anxiety goes hand in hand with other difficulties:

✔ Feeling low or depressed.

✔ Troubled sleep.

✔ Blaming yourself or feeling responsible for bad outcomes.

✔ Drinking too much.

✔ Over-using prescription anxiety medication.

You may find that other problems lift as you overcome your anxiety, but if they're sticking around and complicating your recovery then read on to do something about them.

Dealing with depression

Some people with anxiety also suffer from problems of low mood or depression. Which comes first isn't always clear. For some people, a period of low mood leads to feeling anxious; for others, feeling blue is a consequence of struggling with anxiety for a long time; and sometimes the two seem to have gone together all along.

Here are signs of depression to watch for:

- ✔ Feeling down or hopeless.

- ✔ Having little interest or pleasure in things you used to enjoy.

- ✔ Feeling bad about yourself.

- ✔ Having sleeping difficulties.

- ✔ Lacking energy.

- ✔ Eating more, or less.

- ✔ Struggling to concentrate.

- ✔ Feeling sluggish or, conversely, hyper-activated and restless.

- ✔ Thoughts of death or feeling that you no longer care if you live or die.

If you've been experiencing a number of these symptoms in the last two weeks or more, and they've been intense enough to interfere with your daily life, we recommend that you visit your doctor.

Sometimes when people are depressed, they get so desperate that they think about harming themselves. If you feel this way, remember that help is available – seek help from your doctor.

Tackling your depression may leave you feeling more confident to overcome your anxiety. You can find out more about depression and how to overcome it from *Managing Depression with*

CBT For Dummies by Brian Thomson and Matt Broadway-Horner (Wiley).

The National Institute for Health and Clinical Excellence (NICE), recommend that where people meet diagnostic criteria for both depression and anxiety, then depression should be treated first. Discuss this point with your healthcare professional if you have both problems.

Getting a good night's sleep

Anxiety and trouble with sleeping are often bed fellows. You may find it difficult to get to sleep or stay asleep because of worries running around in your head. Alternatively, you may be jittery, jumpy and woken up too easily and find it difficult to get back to sleep. Disturbed sleep can make you feel tired, uneasy and less able to cope the following day, which perpetuates anxiety.

Practising healthy sleep habits improves your chances of getting a good night's sleep and waking fresh and ready to enjoy your day:

- **Do daytime activities that help promote good sleep.** Getting some exercise during the day helps you to get a better sleep at night. If you can exercise early, do something vigorous. If you need to exercise late, something gentle and de-stressing (walking, yoga, gentle cycling) is more likely to promote better sleep. Exercise outdoors if you can (outdoors is more energising), and in a social group if that suits you.

- **Cut back on caffeine.** Coffee, tea (including green tea) and many cola drinks can contain *caffeine*, a stimulant that can stay in your system for several hours and make it difficult to get to sleep. Avoiding caffeinated drinks after lunchtime helps your body to wind down before bedtime.

- **Say no to a night-cap.** Many people believe that having a night-cap will help them get to sleep. However, drinking alcohol doesn't really encourage good-quality sleep and is likely to lead to interrupted sleep and early waking. If you're having trouble sleeping, cutting back on alcohol can help get you back on track.

✔ **Set up a sleep schedule.** The body responds well to routine. Going to bed and getting up at the same time every day and avoiding daytime napping is the best routine for most people. Try to set a reasonable time to hit the hay and see what happens when you wake up naturally without an alarm clock – try this on a few consecutive days when you don't have to be anywhere too early to find your optimum sleeping time. Then adjust your bed- and wake-time to meet your needs. You may need a couple of weeks to get used to a new routine, but when you find the pattern that works for you, you should get a better night's sleep.

✔ **Relax into a bedtime routine.** Make time before you plan to go to bed to relax yourself towards sleep. Find something that works for you – dimmed lights, an easy read, a warm bath, a milky drink. Treat yourself to this time to wind down and you'll be rewarded with better rest.

✔ **Make your bedroom a haven for sleep.** Your sleeping environment can significantly impact on the quality of your sleep. Promote good sleep by having a place to lay your head that's soft, soothing and free from noise and clutter. Enhance the space with pleasant smells that you associate with good sleep. If you've had trouble sleeping, try changing your pillow or cover arrangements – doing something different can improve your sleeping experience.

✔ **Put sleep in its place.** Avoid lying in bed awake for too long, or doing activities other than sleep and sex in bed. If you watch TV, play computer games, eat your dinner or do puzzles in bed, your brain makes an association between being in bed and being awake – and this association won't help you sleep. If you aren't sleeping, get out of bed and do something else instead – make it something restful or even boring to help wind down your body and mind until you're ready for bed.

✔ **Be sensible about sleep.** Your beliefs about sleep and expectations for a good night's sleep affect how you feel about sleep and your sleep behaviour. Worrying that you won't ever get to sleep, or that you won't cope if you don't get eight hours' sleep doesn't help you get to sleep and is likely to leave you feeling wide-eyed and distressed. Different people need different amounts of sleep, and the amount changes during your life. Trying hard to get to sleep won't help you to relax. Let sleep happen without expectations – you may find that sleep can surprise you.

Being realistic about responsibility

It's good to be good, but it's not always possible. Many people are brought up with the idea that each person has a moral responsibility to do good, but some people take this general rule to the extreme. Having an exaggerated sense of responsibility for the outcome of events that are beyond your control can keep a vicious cycle of anxiety going.

Here's a process that helps you identify whether exaggerated responsibility is an issue for you, and discover a neat way to re-balance feelings associated with exaggerated responsibility:

1. **Bring to mind a recent event that you feel bad about and feel responsible for.**

   You may choose something that didn't work out how you expected or went wrong in some way, or an event in the future that you're worrying about.

2. **Estimate how much you're responsible for this event.**

   Rate on a scale of 0–100, where 0 means not responsible at all and 100 means wholly responsible for the outcome.

3. **Make a list of all the different factors that could influence the outcome of that event.**

   Ask yourself:

   - Who else is involved?

   - What specific circumstances may contribute to the outcome? For example, was the task difficult? Did you have everything you needed to do it well?

   - Can general circumstances, such as the weather or time of day, influence events?

   List all the possible factors. Write everything you think of down, even if you aren't sure that they play a role, or think that they only contributed a little bit.

4. **Complete a pie chart showing the contributing factors.**

Make each contributing factor a slice of a size roughly equivalent to how much that factor is responsible for the outcome. Leave yourself until last, then claim your slice of the pie chart. Figure 8-1 shows an example pie chart where the worry is that your presentation may let your company down, and the company will miss out on an important contract.

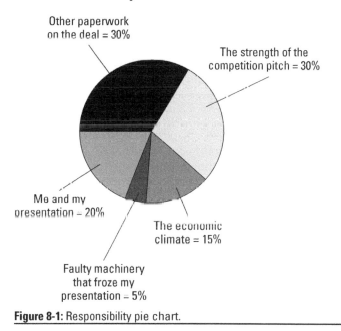

Other paperwork on the deal = 30%

The strength of the competition pitch = 30%

Me and my presentation – 20%

The economic climate = 15%

Faulty machinery that froze my presentation – 5%

Figure 8-1: Responsibility pie chart.

5. Looking at your completed pie chart, how responsible do you now feel for this event?

Rate again from 0–100. Is the figure lower than before? Did completing this exercise have any impact on how you feel about this event?

If you feel relief that you're not wholly responsible for something that you've felt bad about, that's good – but it also suggests that you were carrying exaggerated responsibility for this event to start with. Working on a few more of these charts can help you to recognise and re-balance your realistic level of responsibility.

You're responsible for your own actions, but few events are caused by the actions of a single person alone. Be realistic about your influence on events.

Choosing not to drown anxiety in drink

The emotional and physical experience of anxiety can be really unpleasant. No one likes feeling really unpleasant, so unsurprisingly some people who dislike feeling anxious limit the emotional and physical experience of anxiety with drink.

People who experience a lot of anxiety are more likely to engage in problematic drinking than their less anxious peers. In particular, the association between social anxiety (the fear of social situations where you may feel evaluated or scrutinised by other people) and problem drinking is well established. Feeling anxious, for example before a party or a presentation, some people take a drink as a coping strategy, believing it will boost their confidence – and over time the drinking may just become a habit.

Having a drink or two can feel like it takes the edge off your anxiety in the short term, but the sedative effect is unlikely to build your social skills or confidence and is likely to make you feel more anxious in the longer term. Research suggests that people who are less anxious actually drink less (not more) in response to feeling embarrassed – and it may be that their beliefs about the benefits of alcohol differ from their more anxious friends.

When you've had too much to drink, you don't feel great the following day. The physical consequences of alcohol, including dehydration and depletion of the feel-good brain chemical serotonin, can leave you feeling low in mood, achy, nauseous, dizzy, hazy and confused. As well as being generally unpleasant, these kinds of sensations are exactly the triggers for thoughts that can provoke anxiety and panic.

Are you drinking too much? The following are the recommended limits:

- ✔ **Men:** 21 units in total per week, and not regularly more than 3–4 units a day.

- ✔ **Women:** 14 units in total per week, and not regularly more than 2–3 units a day.

One unit is 10 millilitres of pure alcohol, which is equivalent to half a pint regular strength beer (3.5 per cent alcohol), half a glass of wine (12 per cent alcohol, 175-millilitre glass) or a single spirit shot (25 millilitres).

Whether drinking is a coping strategy or has become a habit, consider cutting back or cutting it out for the sake of overcoming your anxiety and for your health generally.

Cut out illicit drugs. Drugs that you may believe boost confidence, such as amphetamine and cocaine, are actually associated with increased anxiety and even paranoia, and generally lead to lower, rather than higher social competence.

Avoiding over-reliance on anxiety medication

Your doctor may prescribe anxiety medication (benzodiazepines) for the short-term relief of anxiety. They're usually recommended for use over two to four weeks only. Longer-term use of benzodiazapines for anxiety results in reduced effectiveness and can cause addiction – therefore, such longer-term use isn't recommended. Doctors may consider other medication options in the case of specific anxiety diagnoses.

Some people find anxiety medication helpful in coping with the symptoms of anxiety in the short term, but using the cognitive-behavioural strategies in this book can help you to tackle the cause of anxiety rather than just the symptoms.

If you've been taking anxiety medication for a long time and would like to reduce your intake, speak to your healthcare professional who can advise you on how best to cut down and then cut out their use. But don't suddenly stop or change your use of anxiety medication without advice.

Embracing Healthy Living

Taking care of yourself physically, emotionally and socially can all help you to feel good and keep on top of anxiety.

Make a 'taking care of me' kit – a list of the things you find work best for you to keep a healthy balanced body and mind – and then make it a priority to use it. You might include spending time with friends every week, doing an active hobby that you enjoy and making time for a few good nights' sleep. Go on – you're worth it.

Exercising and being active

Regular exercise lowers anxiety and improves mood. Research studies have shown that people with high levels of anxiety are less likely to exercise regularly, but that introducing a regular, structured exercise programme can have a positive effect on anxiety symptoms and mood.

Make time in your life for physical activity – it doesn't matter what you do, just find something you enjoy and keep doing it!

Maintaining regular exercise may be easier with social support – make connections with new people by joining a local sport club or exercise group.

Keeping stress under control

No one lives a stress-free life, but you can take action to notice when stress is around, take charge of your time and practise healthy habits to keep stress under control:

✔ **Know the power of 'no'.** If you're feeling stressed because you're taking on too much at work or in your home life, just say 'no'. If you've always taken all tasks on, it may feel difficult to turn some down, but doing so will give you time to focus on your priorities. Practise saying 'no' and take time to notice the benefits. You're pretty great – but you can't do everything!

✔ **Ask for help.** You're not a superhero – sometimes everyone needs help. Can someone else do a chore you don't have time for, or help you to manage your priorities by pushing a deadline back?

✔ **Relax.** Walk, read, dance, play. Some people find specific relaxation or meditation exercises helpful to manage stress and increase resilience.

Take a look at *Mindfulness For Dummies* and *Relaxation For Dummies*, both by Shamash Alidina (Wiley) on ways to combat stress.

Being a happy eater

Healthy eating isn't about following any diet strictly, but adopting basic healthy principles and enjoying a bit of what you fancy in moderation. You can easily find advice on what constitutes a healthy diet – plenty of fruit and veg, some protein and whole grains – eaten regularly and in sensible amounts (enough to maintain a healthy body weight).

People who typically eat a healthy diet report better mental health than those whose plates are characterised by fried, refined and processed foods. Experts don't yet know whether healthy eating leads to a healthy mind or vice versa, but keeping a balanced healthy diet is a positive step towards well-being.

Also watch your alcohol intake; see the earlier section 'Choosing not to drown anxiety in drink'.

Giving up the cigarettes

People with high levels of anxiety are more likely to smoke than their peers. Health professionals don't yet know whether smokers are more likely to become anxious or people who are anxious tend to start to smoke. Either way, smoking has numerous negative consequences for your health, your relationships and your wallet.

If you're thinking about quitting smoking, check out the National Health Service guidance at `http://smokefree. nhs.uk`.

Doing more enjoyable things

Being anxious takes up a lot of time. As you overcome anxiety, you may find that you've more time and more confidence to do more activities, including new ones. Doing more enjoyable activities in turn improves your mood, builds your confidence and strengthens your resilience against anxiety.

Make a list of things that you'd like to do – things you already know that you enjoy and new things you'd like to give a test-run. Ensure that you include a range of different things on your list – something active, something creative, treats and challenges, both sensible and silly activities. Include at least one thing that you've always wanted to do but have been too anxious to try – and then try it! Here's an example list:

- ✔ Go swimming once a week.
- ✔ Take life-drawing class.
- ✔ Learn French.
- ✔ Book a massage.
- ✔ Make something or fix something in your home.
- ✔ Call a friend, just for a chat.
- ✔ Make time to watch a funny movie.
- ✔ Play an instrument.

- ✔ Go to the zoo.
- ✔ Sign up for a charity fun run or football match.
- ✔ Try a ballroom or salsa dance class.

Now choose one thing that really appeals to you that you can start this week – draw a circle around it. Make a specific plan for doing this activity (where and when will you do it?), and commit yourself to it – write it on the notice board, book in, sign up.

Great ideas don't jump off the page and start doing themselves. You may find that you have doubts about embarking on something new for the first time, but you're likely to find you have more fun than you think that you will!

Maintaining fulfilling relationships

The association between relationships and health is well-established. Both the quantity and quality of relationships we have is a powerful predictor of mental and physical well-being. Spending time with friends, family and significant others is a positive step towards a healthy lifestyle.

Being with friends and family

Friends and family can be an excellent source of support and help to build up your resilience to stress.

Have a number of friends with whom you can enjoy activities and share confidences. But more isn't always better – you can juggle only so many friends. For most people, having 100 Facebook friends isn't as good as one friend that you can really talk to.

If anxious avoidance has limited your social activities, overcoming your anxiety and staying healthy may mean making more connections with others. Find someone you trust with whom you can have frequent contact – meet up regularly to talk, listen, laugh and learn together.

Make a list of people that you could enjoy spending more regular time with. Choose someone from that list and arrange to meet up with them during the next week.

Get in contact with friends and family you've lost touch with and make new connections whenever you can. Join a club, group or class – you open the door to people who share your interests or your enthusiasm for something new.

As you begin to understand and overcome your anxiety, you may notice that anxiety runs in your family or around your friendship group. Perhaps your parents, siblings or friends also tend to worry a lot or avoid certain things? Don't get drawn into others' anxious ideas. Recognising anxiety in other people may help you to better understand how your anxiety developed or has been maintained. Take a step back from other people's anxiety and stay anxiety free.

Considering significant others

Anxiety can cause problems in relationships because it can manifest itself in neediness, suspiciousness and even impulsive behaviour. As you overcome your anxiety, you may also find that your relationship improves too. Notice this improvement and make time to talk about things that are important to each of you.

If you've been anxious for a long time – perhaps all the time your partner has known you – overcoming your anxiety may come as a surprise or even a shock to your partner. Good communication can help you to maintain a good relationship through these changes.

Seize the day. Embrace your new confidence with your partner. If your anxiety has stopped you from going to places or doing things that you may enjoy together – try them now. Visit somewhere special or learn something new together – a sport, craft or skill.

Chapter 9

Creating Your Route Map for a Brighter Future

*W*hen you've worked so hard to overcome fears and anxieties, recognising your achievements and reminding yourself of how far you've come are important. But you don't want this exercise to be a one-off. You want a way to ensure that you continue to move forward with your hopes and dreams.

This chapter helps you to develop a new plan that enables you to monitor your continued success and reminds you of those strategies that worked so well in overcoming your difficulties. We also help you to think about those possible pitfalls and consider what else you'd like to achieve in the future.

Recognising Your Progress

In Chapter 2 we help you map your anxiety, and in Chapter 3 we help you set goals. Now, in this section, we help you analyse your progress against the map and the goals. You become familiar with those strategies that worked well for you and those that perhaps weren't quite so helpful. You identify where your strengths are, and maybe discover some you didn't realise you had! You also find out how best to help those around you.

Seeing where you started and how far you've come

Just look at how far you've come! Through following some of the steps and strategies in the previous chapters, you've found out more about your fears, anxiety or worries. And we hope that you've taken some steps to change how you deal with these difficulties, through changing the way you think, changing the way you behave, or both! You may even feel that you've overcome your difficulties and are looking forward to a time without them.

Have a look at the map we guide you to make in Chapter 2. Look at the triggers that caused you to feel anxious or worried, what happened in your body when you felt that way and then what you did as a result of those feelings and anxieties or worries.

Now have a look back at your SMART goal(s) (we help you to determine these goals in Chapter 3). What did you want to achieve? Think about the hard work and courage you needed to try to achieve your goal, and what strengths and resources you used alongside your strategies.

Finally, review your strategies. Did you try to meet your fears head on, by doing things differently, or did you try to think differently about things that troubled you, or maybe you tried a combination of both!

You may have achieved your SMART goal, you may have come close but not quite got there, or you may have just started to make those changes in the way you behave or think. However much or little progress you feel you've made, it's still progress! Even if you're just *considering* thinking or behaving differently and haven't quite managed to take action yet, you're still in a different place than you were before you started considering.

Updating your map

In Chapter 2 we help you map your anxiety. Take a look at your map and ask yourself the following questions:

- What are my anxiety triggers now?
  - Are they the same?
  - Have the number of triggers reduced?
- What about my anxious thoughts:
  - Do I have as many?
  - Are they so frequent?
  - Am I troubled as much as I used to be by them?
- How do I feel now?
  - Do I get as anxious or worried as I used to?
  - How does my body react now?
- What do I do differently now?
  - What do I do now that I didn't used to do?
  - What have I stopped doing that used to be unhelpful?
- What strengths and resources did I use and how did they help me to tackle my difficulties?

Dodging Pitfalls

You've come a long way; wouldn't you love to keep moving forward? But each day is different and you don't always feel as strong as you'd like to feel or as able to tackle your difficulties as you did the previous day. That's normal! You're bound to have times when you feel that the progress you've made slips back a little. So what you need to think about is what can get in the way of continuing your progress.

Pitfalls can come along in all sorts of guises. You won't be able to avoid all the things that may trigger anxiety, and it wouldn't be helpful if you did! What you can do, however, is to try not to slip back into the previous patterns of thinking or behaving that maintained your anxieties or worries.

Overcoming anxiety can be challenging. Your journey to this point may have had some twists and turns, you might have ended up in cul-de-sacs and had to retrace your steps and try a different way, and at times life may have come along and got in the way of your progress. Don't worry; that's normal.

Knowing what could trip you up

Take a piece of paper and make a list of all the things that have got in the way, or may get in your way, while you've been trying to overcome your difficulty. Taking a look at Chapter 2 can help here – think about a potential pitfall as a trigger and consider how it may then affect the way you feel, think and behave.

Daniel was worried about rats and this worry led him to avoid all sorts of situations in which he thought he could come across rats. Daniel overcame his fear of rats by facing them and associated situations and behaviours in a graded way and no longer avoided many of the situations he used to avoid. Table 9-1 outlines a pitfall to Daniel's great progress.

Table 9-1	Daniel's Pitfall
Trigger	Daniel's daughter Ruth came home from school saying that she had agreed to look after the class pet rat for the half term holiday.
Emotion	Daniel suddenly felt very anxious.
Body sensation	Daniel's heart started to race, his body temperature started to rise and he started to sweat.
Thought	Daniel's first thought was, 'I can't be in the house, the rat might escape; I have to get out.'
Behaviour	Daniel had a strong urge to leave the house, get in the car and drive away.

Sasha used to worry about germs on her hands and on the surfaces of her house. She worried that her family would become poorly if she didn't clean all the time. After learning how to find alternatives to her unhelpful way of thinking about germs, learning that she didn't need to feel totally responsible for the welfare of everyone who came into her house and facing some of her fears, Sasha was able to stop worrying about germs and spent less time cleaning. Table 9-2 shows Sasha's pitfall.

Table 9-2	Sasha's Pitfall
Trigger	Sasha's friend Jess phoned to say she was visiting with her new baby.
Emotion	Sasha suddenly felt anxious.
Body sensation	Sasha noticed that her body became tense and her palms started to sweat. Her throat became dry and her legs wobbly.
Thought	Sasha's first thought was, 'I must clean the house from top to bottom, what if Jess's baby becomes sick after she has visited?'
Behaviour	Sasha had a strong urge to finish the phone call quickly and start cleaning.

Mary used to worry about all sorts of things. She worried whether she could pay her bills, she worried that her husband might have an accident at work, she worried about her grand-children, and whether she would stay well enough to care for them in the future. She thought that if she tried to think about everything that may go wrong, then she would be prepared for any eventuality. After learning that spending so much of her time worrying just made her more worried, and identifying strategies for problem-solving those things she could do something about and letting other worries go, Mary became much more relaxed and was able to pursue her hobbies with-out getting distracted by worry. However, Mary encounters a pitfall, as shown in Table 9-3.

Table 9-3	Mary's Pitfall
Trigger	Mary's husband, Karim, wasn't home at the usual time from work.
Emotion	Mary started to worry.
Body sensation	Mary felt her body become tense and her mouth go dry.
Thought	Mary's first thought was 'What if Karim has had an accident?', followed by 'What if he's been seriously injured and he wasn't carrying his phone?'.
Behaviour	Mary started to think of all the things that may have happened and had a strong urge to ring the hospital and the police.

All these examples show how easily old ways of thinking and feeling can be triggered, and how easily you can fall back into old unhelpful behaviours. Things that happen in your every-day life can trip you up and catch you out, but being mindful of these triggers and things that may make you more vulner-able to these triggers, such as illness, tiredness and stress, mean that you're more likely to be able to dodge the pitfalls.

Watching out for triggers

You have a list of things that may trip you up in your journey to overcome anxiety. Now have a look at the triggers.

Take a look at Table 9-4. On a piece of paper, write:

✔ As many possible triggers (situations in which you may become anxious, fearful or worried) as you can think of.

✔ The strategies from the previous chapters that have helped you to manage or overcome your anxieties. Think about which strategies may work best in which situation.

✔ Your strengths and resources, not forgetting to include all the achievements you've made to date in working to overcome your difficulties.

Table 9-4   Managing Anxiety Triggers

Triggers: Situations, events or things which may cause you to become anxious.

Strategies I have learned

Strengths

Resources

Continuing the examples of Daniel, Sasha and Mary from the previous section, think about how they could do things differently following the work they had done on their difficulties, this time concentrating on their thoughts and behaviour and noticing the effect on their anxiety and worries.

After Daniel's daughter brought home the school's pet rat, Daniel had become anxious and had a strong urge to escape from the situation. Daniel realised that his body was showing a 'flight, fight or freeze' reaction (refer to Chapter 2) and he decided to find alternatives to his thoughts and reminded himself that he had learned he didn't have to be afraid of rats. He then took a deep breath and asked his daughter to tell him about the rat. Over the next couple of hours Daniel was able to go close to the cage without feeling anxious. He reminded himself that just because he had become anxious, it didn't mean that he was back to square one and in fact it was a good opportunity to practise facing his fear.

Sasha's friend phoned to say she was visiting with her new baby. Sasha became anxious and worried and had a strong urge to clean.

Sasha recognised that her old urges were re-emerging and knew that it was important to resist the urge. She reminded herself that the more she gave into the urge, the more she had to clean, but resisting it meant that the anxiety gradually reduced and she was able to find alternatives to her worrying thoughts. When her friend came to visit with the baby, Sasha was able to enjoy seeing her friend without having cleaned excessively beforehand.

Mary's husband, Karim, wasn't home at the usual time from work and Mary started to imagine that something had happened to her husband. She had become anxious and had the urge to phone the hospital and police.

Mary realised that she was slipping back into an old pattern of worrying and that, when she did this, her worries spiralled and made her feel anxious and want to find ways to reassure herself, which never worked effectively. Mary decided that she would get on with cooking the dinner, put on some music and decided to review the situation again in an hour if her husband still wasn't home. Mary involved herself in cooking the dinner and listening to music and before she knew it, her husband had arrived home.

You may not be able to avoid triggers, and you're bound to get stressed, tired and poorly from time to time. If you accept that triggers may well crop up from time to time, you can do something about putting plans in place to reduce their impact.

Planning For a Brighter Future

Although you can't completely avoid triggers of anxiety and worry in the future, as we explain in the previous sections, you can manage and reduce anxieties or worries that may have previously caused you distress. In this section, we think about practical ways to bolster your confidence and integrate these new ways of thinking and behaving into your life.

Giving yourself credit

When you've worked so hard at trying to overcome a difficulty, you must recognise your achievements and the attributes and talents you possess that have helped you make these achievements.

Encouraging self-statements can help give you a boost and keep you going. You may not be used to paying yourself compliments, but give it a try. Here are a few examples:

- 'I've done really well in being able to face my fear.'
- 'Giving up my worrying is hard but I'm working hard each day on trying.'
- 'I've done brilliantly!'
- 'I can achieve this!'

Write five encouraging self-statements. If you find this idea difficult, ask a friend to help you, or think about what you'd say to a friend if she'd achieved the things you had and you wanted to help her to move forward.

Planning your route map

You need a plan that carries you forward from now and consolidates your progress so far. The following is a way you can think about planning your route map.

Use the form in Table 9-5 to write your own route map. Here are some pointers for filling in each section:

- ✔ **What am I like when I'm okay?** Think of some words that you or others use to describe you when you're feeling okay. What kinds of thoughts do you have? How would you describe your feelings when you're okay? What happens in your body? Think about the parts of your body that are affected by feeling anxious or worried. What do you do when you're okay?

- ✔ **My triggers:** What situations might trigger your anxieties? Under what circumstances might you become vulnerable to your worries or anxieties (stress, tiredness, illness and so on)?

- ✔ **How would I recognise if I was becoming anxious or worried?** What kinds of thoughts would you start to have? How would you be feeling? What happens in your body when you're feeling anxious? What do you do or have the *urge* to do at these times?

- ✔ **What strategies can I use to help me?** What strategies have you used that have been helpful – for example, facing your fears (see Chapter 4), using thought records and finding alternatives (see Chapter 2 and 7)?

- ✔ **What tips do I need to remember?** For example, try not to avoid things and remember to write down thoughts.

- ✔ **Strengths and resources:** For example, numbers of friends you can call for support. Try adding some encouraging self-statements that remind you how far you've come (see the preceding section).

Table 9-5	My Route Map
This is what I am like when I am ok:	
My triggers:	
How I recognise if I become anxious or worried:	
Strategies I can use to help me:	
Tips to remember:	
Strengths and resources:	

Setting goals for one year from today

You may feel as if you've already achieved a great deal in overcoming some or many of your anxieties or worries. With a plan in place, you can ensure that you spot pitfalls early and find ways round falling into the traps of old ways of thinking and behaving.

In order to be able to continue along your road to success, think about future goals. You know how far you've come to this point, how you used to think, feel and behave, and how you think, feel and behave now. For the next stage in this journey, think about whether you'd like things to continue changing for you.

Answer these questions:

✔ How do you feel now and how would you like to be feeling a year from now?

✔ What kinds of thoughts are you having now and what kinds of thoughts would you like to be having a year from now?

✔ What do you do/not do now and what would you like to be doing/not doing a year from now?

You may find that your answers to each set of 'now' and 'in a year's time' are the same, or you may have found that you still have changes to make. Perhaps you have some new SMART goals you'd like to achieve!

Part IV
The Part of Tens

The 5th Wave   By Rich Tennant

In this part . . .

Here you'll find vital information about using CBT for anxiety and beyond. You'll find ten dos and don'ts for tackling anxiety and ten tips on expanding your horizons and enjoying your life.

Chapter 10

Ten Tips for Tackling Anxiety

*T*ackling your anxiety can take a lot of hard work and courage. Here are ten tips and key ideas for overcoming fears and worries and enlisting support.

Accept That Anxiety Is a Normal Emotion

Don't be anxious about being anxious! Anxiety is a natural reaction to a threat or danger, and as such is experienced by everyone – so you're not alone when you experience anxiety. Anxiety can help you deal with everyday challenges like

✔ Preparing for an interview

✔ Meeting an important person for the first time

✔ Dealing with challenges, such as finding that your bank balance is overdrawn

Try not to fight off your feelings of anxiety. In most cases, anxiety doesn't last long. Say to yourself, 'I accept this anxiety and will continue doing what I must – it's okay to be anxious.'

Know That Anxiety Can't Harm You

Anxiety is associated with a range of mental and physical experiences that are perfectly natural. Don't interpret anxious thoughts and feelings (for example, everything seems threatening and ominous) as signs that you're going crazy, or physical symptoms (for example, you're perspiring and your heart is beating faster) as evidence that you're ill.

Anxiety is an unpleasant feeling, but it can't harm you. Remind yourself of this fact when you feel anxious and tell yourself, 'Even with these feelings, I can do what I need to do.'

Turn to Chapter 1 for more information on how anxiety affects body and mind.

Avoid Avoidance

Avoidance can keep anxiety going. Of course you avoid some activities in life, like crossing roads with your eyes shut. But if you're avoiding an activity or situation that most people think is safe, you need to tackle your anxiety.

Putting yourself into the situations that you fear means that you get more used to them and, over time, anxiety reduces. You may also find that you've overestimated the danger (see the following section). Check out Chapter 4, where we provide a step-by-step approach to tackling fears.

Check That You've Cause to Be Anxious

Anxiety is a natural reaction to a threat or danger. You're behaving perfectly understandably and normally if you feel anxious when you believe that significant threat or danger is around the corner. The trouble is, sometimes what seems like danger isn't actually danger, or the danger may not be as bad as you think. So the question is whether you're overestimating the threat. You need to check your facts.

Here are a few good fact checks to consider:

- ✔ **Specific phobias:** How many people get harmed by the thing you fear? Where, when and how?

- ✔ **Panic attacks:** What are the normal sensations of anxiety and what causes these? What are the differences between anxiety sensations and others that would signal physical disaster?

- ✔ **Social anxiety:** How much do people really notice the things that you fear being judged about, and if they do notice, do they care?

- ✔ **Obsessive-compulsive problems:** Has thinking about bad things ever caused them to happen? How often do bad things happen to people who don't check or take precautions as much as you do?

- ✔ **Health anxiety:** What are the *most likely* causes of your symptoms? Can anyone ever be absolutely certain that they don't have a serious illness? How do others live with the uncertainty? What would most people judge to be a reasonable amount of investigations or tests to have?

- ✔ **Worry:** Have you or others found that worry is the most effective way to be prepared or solve problems?

For more on separating fact and fiction, including experiments to test whether the worst will happen, head to Chapter 5.

Turn Pointless Worry into a Plan

Worrying isn't the best way to solve problems because it's repetitive, doesn't lead to solutions and spreads into new topics in a disorganised way. Problem-solving and planning are good, focused ways to solve problems that are much more efficient. Whenever you can, turn worry about something that may or may not happen into a concrete plan.

Here are some example plans for addressing different sorts of worries:

- ✔ **Worries about money:** Plan a budget and try to stick to it. Build up savings for times when money is short. Go for financial or debt advice.

- ✔ **Worries about health:** Consult your doctor if you need to. Do what you can to be fit and healthy by stopping smoking, drinking less alcohol, eating healthily and taking regular exercise (for more on well-being, head to Chapter 8).

- ✔ **Worries about relationships:** Work out what would need to happen for the relationship to improve – what you would like to do and what you would like others to do. Talk it over with the person concerned.

- ✔ **Worries about daily hassles and tasks:** Make a list of what you need to do and put timescales against each item. Be realistic, but don't put everything off. Plan what you're going to tackle first. Can you delegate anything or ask someone to help you out?

Want to explore worry further? Take a look at Chapter 6.

Live with Some Uncertainty and Risk

Uncertainty and risk are crucial to any adventure. Can you live life as an adventure, rather than trying to avoid risk and uncertainty? You may as well embrace uncertainty and risk, because avoiding them entirely is impossible!

Most anxiety problems keep going partly due to attempts to control risk and uncertainty. To counteract this, can you do one adventurous thing every day or every week?

Here are some examples of adventurous things you can try:

- ✔ Going into situations where you don't know what's going to happen.

- ✔ Dropping your normal *safety behaviours* (behaviour that you think may keep you safe, explained in detail in Chapter 5).

- ✔ Doing something even though it makes you anxious, if most people would consider it safe.

- ✔ Staying in a situation if most people would consider it safe, rather than escaping.

- ✔ Waiting to discover the outcome rather than trying to get certainty straight away.

- ✔ Reassuring yourself rather than seeking reassurance from others.

- ✔ Acknowledging that you may not know what's going to happen, then letting go of worries rather than arguing with them.

Give Yourself a Break from Unreasonable Rules

'Should', 'must' and 'ought' statements applied inflexibly to yourself, other people or the world around cause a great deal of distress. Demanding the very highest standards of all things, all the time, is a recipe for feeling inadequate and disappointed. No one is perfect! Taking a more flexible view helps you adapt to changing circumstances.

Notice when anxiety rules make unreasonable demands of you or others ('I must never let anyone down', 'I should get the highest grade in all my classes', 'Other people ought to be courteous at all times', 'Life should be fair') and replace these rules with more forgiving and realistic expectations. Hold dear your personal values and preferences by all means, but be reasonable with yourself and others and take a break from rigid rules that cause distress.

For more on the rule-breaking, go to Chapter 7.

Refuse to Let Anxiety Hold You Back

Don't put off doing the things that you want to do just because you feel anxious. You're normal if you reason that feeling anxious is a sign not to move forward, but taking up challenges with anxiety leads to more enriching and rewarding experiences and helps you overcome your anxiety to boot. To overcome anxiety, you need to practise doing things that do initially make you feel anxious, to notice what happens when you test out your predictions (refer to Chapter 5) and to prove your anxiety wrong. This won't happen if you don't make a start.

Taking challenges, doing activities that you value and problemsolving for a happier, healthier life improves your mood and builds your resilience against anxiety in the longer term. As the famous self-help saying goes, feel the fear and do it anyway!

Enlist Help with Change

Talk to friends and family about your plans for tackling your anxiety. Think about how people around you can assist your progress and agree ways in which you can work together. You may want to have a helpful friend or family member read this book too.

Agree which things others can help you with and what you need to do on your own.

Sometimes others helping you can actually turn out to be unhelpful. For example, asking for, and being given reassurance, may prevent you facing your fear or finding more helpful ways to think about a situation. Asking someone to go to the shops for you if you're scared to go yourself might stop you finding out that you can learn to go to the shops without being anxious.

Get Help from a Professional CBT Therapist If You Need It

As much as you may want to tackle your anxieties or fears on your own, sometimes people need a bit more support. If you've tried all the techniques available in this book, looked at changing your thoughts and behaviours, reconstructed your unhelpful thoughts and faced your fears, but have been left still feeling anxious, we suggest you seek professional help.

Ask yourself the following questions:

- ✔ Do I still feel distressed?
- ✔ Would I benefit from more support with tackling this difficulty?
- ✔ Did the techniques I tried help a little, but still leave me with the difficulties?
- ✔ Have I got stuck into unhelpful ways of thinking or behaving that this book doesn't address?

If the answer to any of these questions is yes, we recommend that you seek help from a CBT therapist. Professional CBT help should be available in your area privately or through your local health services accessed via your GP.

Seeking professional help doesn't mean that you've failed, just that you need a little more support with tackling your anxiety.

Chapter 11

Ten Inspiring Tips for Moving On from Anxiety

. . . .

In This Chapter

▶ Trying new things

▶ Boosting your mood with kindness

▶ Looking after your health

▶ Making room for fun

. . . .

Tackling your anxiety is only the beginning. Here are ten top tips to help you improve your life.

Reclaim a Lost Interest

Grab a pen and paper and find somewhere quiet where you won't be disturbed for the next ten minutes or so. As best you can, cast your mind back to a period when you felt really happy or secure in your life and ask yourself:

✔ What did I enjoy doing?

✔ What did I find interesting?

✔ What did I find meaningful?

As answers come to mind, write them down; don't worry if they don't seem relevant to now, just make a note of them all. And don't panic if nothing comes to mind, just move on to the next step.

Now, bring to mind other happy or secure times and ask yourself the same questions and note down any answers.

When you've finished, sit back and review the list. Circle all the activities that sound interesting, enjoyable or meaningful now. Are any of the circled answers things that you can do, but aren't currently doing? If so, why not restart one or more of these activities that you used to enjoy?

Making time to do something you enjoy every day, even if only for a few minutes, can have a positive impact on your mood.

Do Something New

Is there something you've always wanted to do, but have never got round to? Or perhaps friends or family have said you'd really enjoy something, but you've never tried it? Why not make the time now to take up something new? Here are some ideas:

- Eat a new style of food.
- Join a club.
- Start a hobby.
- Take a course.
- Travel somewhere you haven't been before.
- Try a new sport.

Discovering new things that you enjoy adds pleasure and richness to your life. If, however, you're scared to start something new, you can apply the techniques from the previous chapters in this book to help overcome your anxiety.

Act Like Someone You Respect

Think of someone you respect who deals with adversity in a calm and effective way. It can be someone you know personally, someone famous, someone from history, someone fictional or someone who has spiritual meaning for you. If possible, choose someone who has calmly and skilfully responded to challenging situations. Ask yourself:

✔ What is it about this person that I respect?

✔ In what ways do I want to be more like this person in my everyday life?

Then, when you're facing a challenging or difficult situation, ask yourself: what would this person do? And, if it seems helpful, act as they would as best you can. Afterwards, take time to reflect on the difference that acting in this way has made. Was the outcome better? If it was, then why not act in this way again when faced with a similar challenge?

The more you practise your new approach, the more familiar and comfortable it feels.

Make Little Changes for a Big Difference

Make small changes to your everyday routine and notice how they have a knock-on effect elsewhere.

For example, when you're next at the supermarket buy one item you don't normally buy; choose an exotic fruit, a different type of tea, new biscuits, an exciting looking cheese – anything that grabs your imagination! Who knows, your choice may lead to an amazing new dish that you can cook (or alternatively, a disgusting one, but that's okay, you tried something new!).

Here are a few other little changes you can try:

✔ Taking a different route to work.

✔ Reading a newspaper or magazine you don't normally read.

✔ Sitting in a different part of the bus on a daily commute.

✔ Styling your hair a different way.

✔ Changing your shampoo or deodorant.

You really don't have to make a big change, just give those little ones a go and see what happens! Some may not have much effect, but every now and again you may hit on something that makes a significant and positive difference. And the whole process may make life seem just a little more exciting and help you to feel a touch more adventurous and confident.

Sow Seeds of Kindness

Research suggests that carrying out acts of kindness towards others improves mood and has positive consequences for the giver. It can help you feel better about yourself and people are more likely to be kind back to you. So do your best to lend a hand to people and act kindly towards them. Maybe an elderly relative or neighbour would appreciate a visit, perhaps someone at work would value some praise, or you could send an email or card to brighten up someone's day.

Keep a record of the impact of trying these acts of kindness on how you feel and think. And if they seem to be helping, why not plan to continue with them?

Eat Well, Sleep Well, Exercise Well

Looking after your body looks after your mind and supports your mental health. You probably know how to treat your body well: eat a balanced diet, drink alcohol and caffeine in moderation, exercise frequently and regularly get a good night's sleep. However, many people understandably struggle to always make the best choices for their bodies.

As a behavioural experiment, make a small change to your diet, your exercise level or your sleep routine for a week, and see the effect on your mental and physical well-being. For example, you can increase the amount of exercise you do or make realistic changes to your diet. Keep a record of what happens, and, at the end of the experiment, review what impact the changes have had. If you find that the changes help, you can introduce them on a more permanent basis.

For more on well-being, head to Chapter 8.

Develop a Five-year Vision

Having a clear vision of how you'd like your life to progress can help you steer in the direction you want.

Find somewhere where you can sit quietly without being disturbed, close your eyes and imagine that life has gone well and you're five years in the future. Ask yourself:

✔ Where am I living?

✔ What sorts of things am I spending my time doing?

✔ Who am I spending my time with?

✔ What is it that I value most about my life?

On the basis of this experience, develop a vision of how you'd like your life to be in five years. Try to balance realism and hope: the vision needs to be within the realms of possibility, but at the same time optimistic.

Now, break down how you can achieve your vision into manageable steps. If your vision has a number of aspects to it (career, personal life, spiritual life and so on), consider each of these aspects in turn. For each aspect, think about:

✔ What you need to do.

✔ What order you need to do these things.

✔ What resources you can draw on for support; for example, friends and family.

Develop a series of intermediate goals. For example, you may want a change in career, but need to retrain in order for this change to be realistic. Signing up for retraining can be an early goal in your plan.

Then, just do it! Start at Step 1, and work towards your goals. Be sure to celebrate each intermediate goal that you achieve!

Make Friends with Fun

Anxiety and all its consequences can sometimes rob you of your chance to have more fun in life, but now's the time to make friends again with fun.

Go where fun hangs out. For example, go to a comedy club or show, meet up with friends or family, watch a favourite film, go shopping, read a good book or take part in your favourite sport. Also check out the earlier sections 'Reclaim a Lost Interest' and 'Do Something New', which help you get into fun activities.

In addition, try laughing and smiling at things more and seeing whether you end up actually having more fun (although obviously if you feel too much like a forced version of the Cheshire cat, you may be going too far!).

Get in Touch with Nature

Many people find that being outside in the natural world helps them to feel calmer, more energised and more connected with the world around them. If you know that this is true for you, why not spend more time getting in touch with nature? If you're not sure whether you'll have such an experience, why not give it a try and see what happens?

You can find many ways to get more in touch with nature. For example:

- Go for a walk in the countryside.
- Notice the sun or wind on your face and the living world around you as you walk around town.
- Spend time looking at the stars at night.
- Go for a boat ride on a river or sea.
- Tend to a garden or care for an animal.

Practise Mindfulness

People have been using mindfulness meditation for centuries to help maintain and improve their well-being. Mindfulness practice involves directing your attention to present-moment experience in a kind and gentle way. Scientific evidence supports its effectiveness in reducing anxiety.

Try these resources to help you learn mindfulness:

- ✔ Professor Jon Kabat-Zinn's seminal book *Full Catastrophe Living: Using the Wisdom of Your Body and Mind to Face Stress, Pain, and Illness* (Delta)

- ✔ Professor Mark Williams' self-help guide: *Mindfulness: A practical guide to finding peace in a frantic world* (Piatkus).

- ✔ The bestselling *Mindfulness For Dummies* by Shamash Alidina (Wiley).

- ✔ The Mental Health Foundation's excellent website: `www.bemindful.co.uk`.

So why not learn more about mindfulness and give it a try, to see whether it helps you?

About the Authors

Graham Davey BA, PhD, FBPsS is Professor of Psychology at the University of Sussex, UK. Graham has research interests that extend across mental health problems generally, and anxiety and worry specifically. He has published over 140 articles in scientific and professional journals and written or edited 16 books, including *Psychopathology: Research, Assessment & Treatment in Clinical Psychology; Clinical Psychology; Applied Psychology; Complete Psychology; Worrying & Psychological Disorders; Phobias: A Handbook of Theory, Research & Treatment*. Graham has served as President of the British Psychological Society and is currently Editor-in-Chief of the Journal of Experimental Psychopathology (http://jep.textrum.com/).

Kate Cavanagh BA, DPhil, DClinPsy, PG Dip CBT, is a Senior Lecturer in Clinical Psychology at the University of Sussex, and Honorary Clinical Psychologist in Sussex Partnership NHS Foundation Trust. Her research interests include increasing access to evidence-based psychological therapies and she has been involved in the research, development and implementation of CBT based self-help since 2001. Kate has authored 25 academic articles on topics of cognitive behavioural theory and therapy, and was for several years the Psychological Health columnist for *Top Sante* magazine.

Fergal Jones MA, PhD, PsychD, PG Dip, CPsychol is a Senior Lecturer, Clinical Psychologist and BABCP Accredited Cognitive Behavioural Therapist. He works part time at Canterbury Christ Church University, teaching on clinical psychology and CBT training programmes, and part time in Sussex Partnership NHS Foundation Trust, where he offers CBT and Mindfulness Based Cognitive Therapy to clients and provides supervision to CBT therapists and MBCT teachers. Fergal has contributed to undergraduate clinical psychology textbooks and published a number of research papers. Fergal's clinical work has primarily been with adults with mental health problems and he has a particular interest in mindfulness-based approaches.

Lydia Turner MSc CBT, Dip Adult Behavioural Psychotherapy, RMN is a Consultant Psychological Therapist at Sussex Partnership NHS Foundation Trust and Programme Director for the MSc/PG Dip in Psychological Therapies at the University of Sussex. She has worked as a Cognitive Behavioural Psychotherapist in the NHS for over 20 years with people with a whole range of mental health difficulties, specialising in working with people with complex difficulties, in a clinical, supervisors and consultative role. Lydia has led CBT Masters programmes teaching clinicians how to use CBT with common mental health difficulties and is currently involved in leading the PG Dip in CBT at the University of Sussex.

Adrian Whittington D Clin Psychol, MSc, PG Dip CBT is a Consultant Clinical Psychologist and CBT specialist who leads training for psychologists and psychological therapists at Sussex Partnership NHS Foundation Trust. He has led postgraduate programmes training CBT therapists and other psychological practitioners and specialises in the application of CBT to complex difficulties with anxiety and depression. Adrian regularly speaks about CBT at national conferences, has published papers about psychological therapies and the training of psychological practitioners and has appeared on Radio 4's 'All in the Mind' programme, discussing how CBT might become more widely available.

Dedication

For Kate and Lizzie – Graham

For Mum and David and for Dave – Kate

For Rowan and Hugo – Fergal

For Eileen – Lydia

For Jane, Joshua and Oliver – Adrian

Authors' Acknowledgements

Graham: Thanks to all my co-authors for their invaluable and authoritative contributions to this book, and for being great people to work with.

Kate: Thank you to each of the teachers, supervisors, colleagues, mentors and clients I've known who have helped me to understand and work with anxiety from a cognitive behavioural perspective. In particular, thank you to Kathy Greenwood, who helped me enormously with my writing for this book.

Thanks also to Graham, Lydia, Adrian and Fergal for being a great team to work with.

Fergal: Charlotte Hartley-Jones MA, MSc, PsychD, CPsychol co-authored Chapters 2 and 11. We would like to thank all the therapists, teachers, supervisors and clients who we've learnt our therapeutic skills from. Many of the ideas we have included in our contributions to this book draw on the work of others, including Aaron Beck, Judith Beck, David M. Clark, Christine Padesky, Paul Salkovskis, Nigel Short, Michael White and Adrian Wells.

Lydia: I would like to thank all those people from whom I have learnt useful CBT interventions for anxiety including people who have undertaken therapy with me, Mark Hardcastle, Nick Maguire, Ken Gordon, my CBT colleagues within Sussex Partnership Trust and those authors and researchers whose writings informed my knowledge and practice.

Adrian: Nearly all of the ideas I have drawn on in contributing to this book are not original. Thank you to all the people who I have learnt from about helpful ways of dealing with anxiety, especially Nick Grey, Stirling Moorey, Sheena Liness, David M. Clark, Paul Salkovskis, Blake Stobie, Gillian Butler, Christine Padesky, Roger Smith and all the people with anxiety difficulties who I have worked with in therapy.

Publisher's Acknowledgments

We're proud of this book; please send us your comments at http://dummies.
custhelp.com. For other comments, please contact our Customer Care Department
within the U.S. at 877-762-2974, outside the U.S. at (001) 317-572-3993, or fax 317-572-4002.

Some of the people who helped bring this book to market include the following:

*Acquisitions, Editorial,
and Vertical Websites*

Project Editor: Rachael Chilvers

Commissioning Editor: Kerry Laundon

Development Editor: Charlie Wilson

Assistant Editor: Ben Kemble

Technical Editor: Simon Easton,
Senior Psychology Lecturer,
University of Portsmouth

Proofreader: Kim Vernon

Production Manager: Daniel Mersey

Publisher: David Palmer

Cover Photos: © maxuser / iStockphoto

Cartoons: Rich Tennant
www.the5thwave.com

Composition Services

Project Coordinator: Kristie Rees

Layout and Graphics: Jennifer Creasey,
Erin Zeltner

Proofreader: Jessica Kramer

Indexer: Potomac Indexing, LLC

Index

FOR DUMMIES

Making Everything Easier! ™

UK editions

BUSINESS

978-0-470-97626-5

978-0-470-74737-7

Starting & Running a Business ALL-IN-ONE

978-1-119-97527-4

REFERENCE

978-0-470-68637-9

DIY

978-0-470-97450-6

Dad's Guide to Pregnancy

978-1-119-97660-8

HOBBIES

978-0-470-69960-7

978-1-119-99417-6

978-1-119-97250-1

Asperger's Syndrome For Dummies
978-0-470-66087-4

Basic Maths For Dummies
978-1-119-97452-9

Body Language For Dummies,
2nd Edition
978-1-119-95351-7

Boosting Self-Esteem For Dummies
978-0-470-74193-1

British Sign Language For Dummies
978-0-470-69477-0

Cricket For Dummies
9/8-0-470-03454-5

Diabetes For Dummies, 3rd Edition
978-0-470-97711-8

Electronics For Dummies
978-0-470-68178-7

English Grammar For Dummies
978-0-470-05752-0

Flirting For Dummies
9/8-0-470-74259-4

IBS For Dummies
978-0-470-51737-6

Improving Your Relationship
For Dummies
978-0-470-68472-6

ITIL For Dummies
978-1-119-95013-4

Management For Dummies,
2nd Edition
978-0-470-97769-9

Neuro-linguistic Programming
For Dummies, 2nd Edition
978-0-470-66543-5

Nutrition For Dummies, 2nd Edition
978-0-470-97276-2

Organic Gardening For Dummies
978-1-119-97706-3

12-43522

FOR DUMMIES

Making Everything Easier!™

UK editions

SELF-HELP

Cognitive Behavioural Therapy For Dummies
978-0-470-66541-1

Creative Visualization For Dummies
978-1-119-99264-6

Mindfulness For Dummies
978-0-470-66086-7

STUDENTS

Philosophy For Dummies
978-0-470-68820-5

Student Cookbook For Dummies
978-0-470-974711-7

Sociology For Dummies
978-1-119-99134-2

HISTORY

The Tudors For Dummies
978-0-470-68792-5

Medieval History For Dummies
978-0-470-74783-4

British History For Dummies
978-0-470-97819-1

Origami Kit For Dummies
978-0-470-75857-1

Overcoming Depression For Dummies
978-0-470-69430-5

Positive Psychology For Dummies
978-0-470-72136-0

PRINCE2 For Dummies, 2009 Edition
978-0-470-71025-8

Project Management For Dummies
978-0-470-71119-4

Psychometric Tests For Dummies
978-0-470-75366-8

Renting Out Your Property For Dummies, 3rd Edition
978-1-119-97640-0

Rugby Union For Dummies, 3rd Edition
978-1-119-99092-5

Sage One For Dummies
978-1-119-95236-7

Self-Hypnosis For Dummies
978-0-470-66073-7

Storing and Preserving Garden Produce For Dummies
978-1-119-95156-8

Study Skills For Dummies
978-0-470-74047-7

Teaching English as a Foreign Language For Dummies
978-0-470-74576-2

Time Management For Dummies
978-0-470-77765-7

Training Your Brain For Dummies
978-0-470-97449-0

Work-Life Balance For Dummies
978-0-470-71380-8

Writing a Dissertation For Dummies
978-0-470-74270-9

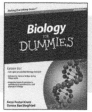

Making Everything Easier!™

COMPUTER BASICS

978-0-470-57829-2

978-0-470-61454-9

978-0-470-49743-2

DIGITAL PHOTOGRAPHY

978-0-470-25074-7

978-0-470-76878-5

978-1-118-00472-2

MICROSOFT OFFICE 2010

978-0-470-48998-7

978-0-470-58302-9

978-0-470-48953-6

Access 2010 For Dummies
978-0-470-49747-0

Android Application Development
For Dummies
978-0-470-77018-4

AutoCAD 2011 For Dummies
978-0-470-59539-8

C++ For Dummies, 6th Edition
978-0-470-31726-6

Computers For Seniors
For Dummies, 2nd Edition
978-0-470-53483-0

Dreamweaver CS5 For Dummies
978-0-470-61076-3

iPad 2 For Dummies, 3rd Edition
978-1-118-17679-5

Macs For Dummies, 11th Edition
978-0-470-87868-2

Mac OS X Snow Leopard
For Dummies
978-0-470-43543-4

Photoshop CS5 For Dummies
978-0-470-61078-7

Photoshop Elements 10
For Dummies
978-1-118-10742-3

Search Engine Optimization
For Dummies, 4th Edition
978-0-470-88104-0

The Internet For Dummies,
13th Edition
978-1-118-09614-7

Visual Studio 2010 All-In-One
For Dummies
978-0-470-53943-9

Web Analytics For Dummies
978-0-470-09824-0

Word 2010 For Dummies
978-0-470-48772-3

WordPress For Dummies,
4th Edition
978-1-118-07342-1

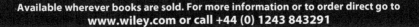